Spiritual
and
Religious

Perspectives
and Context

Rev. Thomas M. Santa, CSsR

T0356604

Catholic. Pastoral. Trusted.

Imprimi Potest: Kevin Zubel, CSsR, Provincial
Denver Province, the Redemptorists

Published by Liguori Publications, Liguori, Missouri 63057

Liguori Publications, a nonprofit corporation, is an apostolate of the
Redemptorists (Redemptorists.com).

Phone: 800-325-9521 *Web:* Liguori.org

Spiritual and Religious: Perspectives and Context
Copyright © 2025 Thomas M. Santa

ISBN 978-0-7648-2871-3
E-ISBN: 978-0-7648-7254-9

Cataloging in Publication data has been applied for with the Library
of Congress

Printed in the United States of America
29 28 27 26 25 / 5 4 3 2 1
First Edition

Cover design: John Krus
Cover illustration: Shutterstock

Dedication

To Dr. Larry Jehling, who encouraged me to take the
time to write this book. His continued friendship and
support have never failed, and I am deeply grateful.
Without his encouragement, this book would have remained just another idea.

About the Author

Rev. Thomas M. Santa, CSsR, is the president and publisher of Liguori Publications, his second assignment as the company's leader. Professed as a Redemptorist in 1973, Fr. Santa has engaged in a variety of ministries, including retreat work; serving for many years as the spiritual director and a pastoral counselor for clients who access the ManagingScrupulosity.com website; and writing reflections and answering reader questions for decades in Liguori Publications' *Scrupulous Anonymous* newsletter.

Author's Note

Some content in *Spiritual and Religious* was previously published as *Christian Contemplative Living: The Essential Connecting Points.* That book is no longer available. This new book is more comprehensive and is a new presentation and position on the topic. More than a revised or updated version, this book presents a different perspective, building on and expanding the original.

Rev. Thomas M. Santa, CSsR

Contents

Introduction   11

CHAPTER ONE
Relationship
The Call to Respond to Mystery   31

CHAPTER TWO
Discipline and Practice
Learning to Focus Attention   71

CHAPTER THREE
Aware and Awake
The Movement from the Less to the More   107

CHAPTER FOUR
Nourishment
Entering Silence and Solitude   139

CHAPTER FIVE
Conversion
A Change in Attitude and Perception   171

CHAPTER SIX
Resurrection
Living the Abundant Life   213

Afterword   245

Bibliography   251

"*These perspectives will appear absurd to those who don't see that life is, from its origins, groping, adventurous, and dangerous. But these perspectives will grow, like an irresistible idea on the horizon of new generations.*"

TEILHARD DE CHARDIN, SJ

Introduction

When I was about nine years old, I was at home during a nondescript morning on a day off from school. With our mother at work and our sitter nearby, my two sisters and I sat quietly on the floor of the living room, trying to occupy ourselves with whatever board game we could manage to play together without fighting.

It was a typical January day in Michigan: overcast and snowing. The weatherman said we were experiencing "lake effect" snow, but it sure looked like it was accumulating at a frantic pace. I remember wondering if I would have to go outside and shovel the driveway soon. This possibility made my attention to the board game more intense, as if my commitment would somehow excuse me from shoveling!

As lunchtime neared, our sitter, a senior in high school, prepared tomato soup and grilled-cheese sandwiches for lunch. This was and remains a perennial favorite lunch (and sometimes dinner). The menu suggests that it must have been a Friday, because that was a traditional lunch when abstinence from meat every

Friday was still a normal penitential requirement in Catholic discipline and practice.

Our regular sitter watched over us to earn some extra cash. In between her assigned duties, she also did her homework. Her textbooks, piled high on the kitchen table, were carefully positioned and ready for her use. Some texts were open to a particular page for study, while others just sat on the table, perhaps for easy reference or in a certain order of importance known only to our sitter.

On this day, I recall that I excused myself from the board game, walked into the kitchen, and, with some effort, pulled myself up onto one of the kitchen chairs near the textbooks. I then took a book to examine it. I don't remember the subject matter, but I recall exactly how I felt as I paged through the text. I was devastated. I was overcome with high anxiety and a sense of impending doom. I didn't understand a thing I read! I recall thinking to myself, *When I get to high school, how am I ever going to be smart enough to understand all this stuff?*

I pushed myself away from the table, climbed down from the chair, returned to my place on the living-room floor, and went back to the game. My sisters probably didn't notice my change in mood, but I most certainly did. The grilled-cheese sandwich and tomato soup did nothing to lighten my disposition. I remained sullen and withdrawn throughout lunch. After eating, I turned down my sister's invitation to resume our game. I excused myself, went upstairs to my bedroom, and remained in my funk for the rest of the afternoon.

When my mother got home from her long day at the office, she busied herself with making dinner, despite being tired. I emerged from my room (but not from my mood), trudged down the stairs, and helped set the table for dinner. As she expertly handled her tasks, she soon sensed something was amiss with me and asked what was going on. When I shared with her my experience with the textbook, she responded by giving me one of those looks that only a mother can give to her son. It seemed to me that she was wondering, *What have I done? Where did this child come from?*

Once she recovered from her surprise, she calmed herself and comforted me. She assured me that when I became a student in high school, I would be well prepared to read and study the assigned texts. She also let me know that few nine-year-olds could understand a high-school textbook, so I should not be too concerned.

Because I knew my mother was trustworthy, I immediately felt relieved and reassured.

I have often recalled this charming childhood episode. I bring it to mind especially at times when I have felt ill prepared to take on a particular task or challenge. To this day, I can easily replay my mother's soothing voice and words of reassurance: "You will be prepared when it is required of you." When I recall the moment and her calm, confident voice, I am inspired and no longer anxious. I understand that if I take each component of the challenge as it unfolds before me, if I connect with the experience as it is revealed, if I resist the urge to try and speed up my pace unnecessarily, in the words of the wise mystic Julian of Norwich: "All will be well."[1]

I have also learned that this memorable encounter with my mother was an example of the tender manifestation of love and trust between a mother and a son— and it was more. In those few minutes, I was mentored by a person who was familiar with the path that was to unfold as I matured. As my mentor, my mother taught me that I would one day acquire the intellectual skills I needed. She knew the path. She had walked it too. And she was able to clearly speak words that I could believe. I was encouraged. Anxiety was replaced with confidence.

As a priest, spiritual director, and retreat director for the greater part of my priesthood, I am often privileged to be invited to share aspects of others' religious and spiritual journeys. When I listen to the personal stories of people of all ages, I am often struck by a common concern. They report a lack of confidence or assurance that they are on the right path. They share that they feel no sense of progress. On occasion, they will also express an inner struggle that gnaws at them. They wonder if they are even capable of engaging in spiritual practice and a religious discipline. They wonder what might happen if they choose, as so many of their friends and even family members have done, to walk away from their traditional religious disciplines and associations. They ask themselves, *If I am not a member of a religious tradition, how can I truly claim to be spiritual? Is it possible or, for that matter, desirable for me to embrace what many now believe: that they are spiritual but not religious?*

Defining that commonly heard description, "spiritual but not religious" (SBNR), is difficult because spirituality is highly personal. Each person has his or her own definition. But I have found that those who identify as

SBNR generally believe in the existence of the divine but have little, if any, interest in organized religion. I hope this simple definition provides some clarity as you read this book.

This topic is important because, time and again, people have shared with me their frustrations and anxieties, often summed up with this sentiment: "Despite my best efforts, I just do not feel close to God. There just seem to be too many contradictions." The feeling of being well and doing well is somehow missing from their own beliefs about their spiritual paths, religious practices, and religious traditions. They experience the anxiety that comes with unease as a necessary first step on the path of discovery.

The good news is that this feeling of unease often enables a change within a person. Some people will embrace this change, while others will ignore what they feel and leave it untested. A not-uncommon response is to reconnect with a newfound intensity and dedication to their familiar religious tradition.

For those who sense a need for change, it will take root with no set pattern or time frame. It can be quick, almost spur of the moment, perhaps in response to a disappointment or a conflict. Change also can take place slowly. Eventually, there is a complete disconnect from religious discipline and practice, and, when acted upon, these are replaced with a vague sense of being spiritual—or, in some instances, a total rejection of any identification or connection with the spiritual.

This new experience is unfamiliar and uncharted, but it produces some feeling of satisfaction. Without the context of their abandoned religious discipline, or even with the severe judgment of their tradition that frowns on anyone walking away from it, people may feel perplexed and overwhelmed. At first, they may feel relief because they have emptied themselves of religion's "strictures." However, for many, they need to fill that void.

At that point, the hard truth is that not everyone will even consider the ramifications of what they have changed, abandoned, or ignored. Some will not commit to filling the emptiness left by leaving "church" behind. "Spiritual but not religious" has become, for many, a defining statement that is acceptable in the prevailing culture to explain or summarize what they might feel or embrace. Those who adopt SBNR often believe nothing else is needed, and they have no intention or desire to be part of any other reality—especially organized religion. The finality that can result from embracing SBNR is enough for many. But SBNR is not the last word for all. For some, it's a beginning. For those who believe that their SBNR perspective is a starting point on their journey, they can find helpful direction.

One way I try to help people get in touch with their experience—even if they feel disconnected—is to encourage them to examine the "big picture." Often, it can help—or at least be reassuring and somewhat comforting—for a person to see something within the context of the larger experience. The bigger picture often provides a glimpse of the path one has already traveled as well as a look at what is ahead down the road. Obviously, this larger examination can only happen if the person makes the effort.

When one looks at the wider view, it is quite possible for him or her to recognize the connecting points: the moments in life when he or she has been squarely positioned at the exact point that was most advantageous at that time. It may come as a surprise for the person to see that he or she has experienced any movement or growth, but it is nonetheless present. A bonus is that with this recognition can come a measure of satisfaction and an impulse to keep moving spiritually.

A spiritual path is one of the roads men and women can walk in life. Not all people will deliberately take this road; other avenues may occupy their attention. However, people who determine they need a spiritual connection will often discover—to their amazement—that they have been unknowingly traveling a spiritual path all their lives. They may not be aware that the path they have been walking has spiritual significance. Even more will be surprised to learn that their spiritual path has definition.

This "surprise" spiritual path may be identified as a form of contemplation in the best and most traditional understanding of the term. Contemplation is more natural to the human person than religious experiences, and the inclination for a person to identify what he or she has contemplated is somehow sacred.

As we will see, there are distinct and essential steps on the spiritual path, although each step is not necessarily seamless, with one following the other in a natural progression. The experience and growing awareness of contemplation does not follow the process of mastering each step before taking the next step on the journey. People do not experience progress as a kind of lesson plan or strategy of living. While there is some sense of having "mastered" a particular step or, in the language of this book, "connecting point," most people experience the connecting points randomly.[2]

This book will review and examine the essential connecting points that people usually encounter as they progress on their spiritual journeys. For you, participation in a practiced religious tradition may well be part of your life. For others, it may not be. Perhaps it once was. Perhaps it never has been. Regardless, a religious tradition and practice does not guarantee a spiritual practice. The reverse is also true: a spiritual practice does not need a religious tradition to be effective, nourishing, and life-giving.

I write as one who is spiritual and religious. My disciplines and practices are rooted in Roman Catholicism, and I will often write from that perspective. At other times, I will challenge both the practice and the tradition of my religion in a manner that is intended to be respectful and appropriate.

I propose that the connecting points as discussed and presented here might best be seen as a way of enabling and recognizing the experience of contemplative living. A contemplative awareness of life is perhaps best experienced as a spiritual practice; it may or may not be associated with a religious discipline. A contemplative life is fully awake and fully alive. Admittedly, the practice of contemplation is a spiritual perspective and understanding of the meaning of human life, and some may struggle with this perspective. Hopefully, this book will help clarify any struggles you may have with it.

This spiritual perspective and understanding would further assert that all people are invited to engage in the gift of life with their eyes wide open, drinking in the wonder and the beauty, in awe of all that surrounds them. This gift of grace leads them to an experience of the sacred, the experience of God, and the manifestation of the "presence of Divine Mystery."[3] Contemplative living nourishes the conditions that are required for an individual person to potentially grow each day in the experience of maturity. It is a new awareness; it is a new way of living and engaging in life.

As people grow and develop through the spiritual practice of contemplative living, they experience what it means to become spiritually mature. Spiritually mature people recognize and somewhat understand the ordinary and even extraordinary experiences of life that connect a man or woman with the singular manifestation of divinity. During this process, the individual will maintain a balance and perspective with each point of connection within the context of a continuing journey.

Another indication of growing and maturing as a spiritual person—and I would assert that it is perhaps the most important indication of maturity—is the sustained ability to maintain a profound respect and reverence for each connecting point as it is experienced. In other words, a spiritually mature person can effortlessly and gratefully experience again and again a point of connection at the beginning stages of the spiritual journey as reverentially as he or she experiences a point that is perhaps more profound.

Although I am unable to identify myself as a completely formed and spiritually mature person, I believe I am growing in the spiritual maturity that comes with the gift of grace. For example, although there are some devotions and pious prayers that I no longer use in my own spiritual practice, I respect and revere their use by others. On the occasions when I am invited to express my spiritual practice in a manner that I no longer routinely use, I do not struggle with the expression but rather maintain a healthy respect for the practice. I recognize that at one time in my life, the practice was an essential experience of my spiritual journey. When

I am invited to share in spiritual practices that demand a more focused and ritualized expression with which I am unfamiliar, I express the practices respectfully. Spiritually mature people accept the grace and power of God in many different experiences and practices. They don't insist on one expression.

As we explore growing in spiritual maturity, we will examine six connecting points in this book; one connecting point is presented in each chapter as follows:

1. Responding to the call of relationship with Divine Mystery

2. Focusing your attention and learning discipline

3. Moving from less to more through awareness

4. Embracing the nourishment of silence and solitude

5. Changing your attitude and perception for true conversion

6. Living the abundant life

I believe that most people will recognize these connecting points as contemplative. Hopefully, this perspective and the identified connecting points will help clarify and deepen your appreciation of the emerging spiritual practice. If you spend time with this book, you may recognize in these connecting points something of what it means to grow in the spiritual life. From my Christian and Catholic perspectives, I also hope that something of the wisdom and teaching of Jesus Christ will be part of your experience.

I anticipate that you will discover a new, and perhaps more satisfying, understanding and appreciation of your own spiritual practice. I believe that if you reflect on the lessons, you will receive much-needed encouragement. May this encouragement enable you to deepen your appreciation of what you need to grow and develop, through the gift and grace of God, into a spiritually mature adult man or woman who embraces a life that is contemplative at its core.

I believe most readers of this book will have a strong religious identity and practice. I also presume that most are familiar with the dogmas and doctrines, the sacraments, the liturgy, the rituals, and the pious devotions and expressions of the Christian life. As you read these pages, notice that I make few direct references to the religious practices and traditions of any specific denomination. Rather, I attempt to build upon the foundational teachings of Jesus, with an emphasis on the spirituality that animates and informs the universal tradition.

You may profit from this book even if you don't belong to an organized and denominational religious tradition. If you seek spiritual direction, this book will help. The spiritual connecting points are grace-filled and for everyone.

My intent is not to assume the role of a teacher but for you to see me as a mentor or trusted companion—someone you want to be with for some reflective moments, help, and reassurance. Although I am a spiritual director and practitioner, it's safe to say I am no saint. But I do feel I understand something of the path that Jesus invited his apostles and disciples to walk. As a result, I believe I can assure and direct.

I aim to encourage you as I invite you to continue your journey. If you have any anxiety, I hope it will be replaced with the confidence my mother once helped instill in me so that you come to believe, as Julian of Norwich wrote, "all will be well."

At the same time, I am aware of my deficiencies and

lack of expertise. I do not pretend that this book is anything more than a small contribution to an ongoing discussion. I am also aware that this book is very limited in scope. Nevertheless, I have been encouraged to write this volume primarily by those who have attended my presentations on these perspectives and the context that makes sense to me in my own experience. The enthusiasm with which these men and women have participated has motivated me to offer this book. If *Spiritual and Religious* contributes something pastoral and useful, then the energy expended will have been well worth the effort.

I suggest you become familiar with the following seven points—my basic methodology for organizing the chapters—before continuing with the book. In so doing, I believe you will get more out of each chapter.

1. **Title:** The theme of each chapter—the connecting point presented—and what is required of you are found in the chapter title.

2. **Quotations:** Passages from Scripture, spiritual masters, and spiritual writers from various tra-

ditions are intended to crystallize the theme of the chapter and help you focus.

3. **Narrative:** The main section of the text reveals the components that are part and parcel of the chapter's theme. Subheads are included occasionally.

4. **Jesus:** The wisdom of Jesus Christ follows the main section, and we look at the chapter's theme in the light of his life, teaching, or mission. This section provides context to the connecting point.

5. **Commentary:** My comments bring context to the theme, complement the theme, and help you apply the theme to your life.

6. **Disconnect:** The last section of each chapter gives an example that examines how someone might disconnect, consciously or unconsciously, from the spiritual path.

7. **Endnotes:** Numerical citations in the text are outlined in a section at the end of each chapter. Additional material and occasional commentary are included.

At the end of the book, I provide a bibliography of the texts I refer to in this book. These texts can be great resources if you'd like to read more about the topics addressed in *Spiritual and Religious.*

I suggest you maintain a reflective posture while reading. Although the text provides material that you can apply to learning and comprehending the perspective and context of what may be broadly identified as "contemplative living," many of the examples will help you reconnect with your own life and perhaps deepen your understanding. A personal connection with a powerful memory, a life experience, or an unanswered question presents opportunities to pause and reflect.

This is your opportunity to learn a lesson or discern a direction for your life. This learning beckons specific reflection, prayer, and gratitude for graces you have received. I urge you to seize such opportunities and celebrate them.

I've also woven references to spiritual direction throughout the book. I believe that spiritual direction and a good spiritual director are essential for the process of growing in spiritual maturity, so I discuss this in various places in *Spiritual and Religious.*

Note: All Scripture quotations used in this book are from *The New American Bible, Revised Edition*, 2010.

Introduction Notes

1. Julian of Norwich (1342–1416) was a significant medieval saint. Her *Revelations of Divine Love* is considered one of the most remarkable documents from this period in history. This mystic was not formally canonized, and her unofficial feast day is celebrated on May 13.

2. It may be helpful to imagine a continuum rather than a straight line. Imagine a "wheel of life" with six connecting points. People connect with individual points on the wheel at different periods in their life and often return to a previous point of connection as the wheel turns.

3. "The presence of Divine Mystery" means "God." The phrase identifies a divine presence while avoiding the word "God." Some associate God more with religion than with spirituality. Readers will view the phrase differently, finding it freeing, limiting, incomplete, or otherwise.

CHAPTER ONE

Relationship

The Call to Respond to Mystery

"Ask and it will be given to you; seek and you will find; knock and the door will be opened to you."

MATTHEW 7:7

"God leads the child he has called in wonderful ways. God takes the soul to a secret place, for God alone will play with it in a game of which the body knows nothing. God says, 'I am your playmate! Your childhood was a companion of my Holy Spirit.'"

MECHTILD OF MAGDEBURG

"To seek is as good as seeing. God wants us to search earnestly and with perseverance, without sloth and worthless sorrow. We must know that God will appear suddenly and joyfully to all lovers of God."

JULIAN OF NORWICH

"Thou takest the pen and the lines dance. Thou takest the flute—and the notes shimmer. Thou takest the brush—and the colors sing. So, all things have meaning and beauty in that space beyond time where thou art. How, then, can I hold back anything from thee?"

DAG HAMMARSKJÖLD, *MARKINGS:*
SPIRITUAL POEMS AND MEDITATIONS

"God's presence accompanies the sincere efforts of individuals and groups to find encouragement and meaning in their lives. He dwells among them, fostering solidarity, fraternity, and the desire for goodness, truth, and justice. This presence must not be contrived but found, uncovered. God does not hide himself from those who seek him with a sincere heart, even though they do so tentatively, in a vague and haphazard manner."

POPE FRANCIS, *EVANGELII GAUDIUM*
(THE JOY OF THE GOSPEL), 71

Relationship with the Divine

A singular, powerful, theological and dogmatic truth[1] within the Christian spiritual tradition is riveting in its assertion and in the ramifications of the pronouncement. The assertion: each member of humanity has been called into life by a Creator God[2] (*Catechism of the Catholic Church*, 199) and as an individual uniquely loved by the Creator. The *Catechism*, quoting the document *Gaudium et Spes* (Joys and Hopes) of the Second Vatican Council, expresses this dogmatic truth in these words: "For if man exists, it is because God has created him through love, and through love continues to hold him in existence" (*CCC* 27).

As if this dogma is not enough, the Christian tradition further insists that the Creator God desires to be intimately in relationship with creation, specifically with humanity. In other words, not only does God love his creation, but God desires also to be loved in return by his creatures. The give and take is active and includes all those qualities that are fundamentally necessary for any other relationship that humans can experience.

For each person who accepts this theological viewpoint as it has been preserved and nurtured in the Christian tradition, there is the ability to join an individual response of belief with the responses of count-less other men and women through the ages who also accept this singular expression of faith with enthu-siasm. Many people, therefore, join their voices with those of the Church when it teaches that "in many ways, throughout history down to the present day, men have given expression to their quest for God in their religious beliefs and behavior: in their prayers, sacri-fices, rituals, meditations, and so forth. These forms of religious expression, despite the ambiguities they often bring with them, are so universal that one may well call man a religious being" (*CCC* 28).

Christian believers assent they are religious beings and believe that statement from the *Catechism* is a rev-elation, or the revealed Word of God. Revelation comes to the people of God through Scripture, tradition, and our observance of the world (Creation). These three components are the "converging and convincing argu-ments" of the order and beauty of the universe (*CCC* 31). As powerful as these components are, there is yet a more compelling argument.

For most people of faith, the ultimate experience that proves to them the presence of Divine Mystery[3] is a per-sonal encounter with the inexpressible but nevertheless convincing presence of a sense of being that they identify as sacred and divine. As Christians, a traditional way to understand and fully appreciate such a personal encounter is to seek further enlightenment about how this type of encounter has been lived out in the past. It is quite helpful to turn to the stories of ancestors in faith to see how they experienced their encounters with the divine. Sacred Scripture is the place to start.

Ancestors in Faith—Old Testament

It is reasonable to believe that people have always wanted to encounter the "other," "divinity," or God. At certain times in history, people were preoccupied primarily with physical survival, so this curiosity was mostly set aside. When they had survival and safety measures in place, the desire was reignited in their imaginations, their feelings, and the deepest parts of themselves. We know this to be true because archeologists have uncovered numerous ruins, paintings, and other artifacts that represent humanity's quest for encountering what I am calling "the presence of Divine Mystery."

Our ancient ancestors looked back at where they had journeyed from and shared stories that captured some of the essence of what they recognized as important. In

35

the many thousands of years of humanity's existence, people have seen manifestations of mystery through form, presence, or elaborate ritual.

It is impossible to pinpoint the first moment in the human journey when someone acted upon the awareness of and desire for a connection with Divine Mystery. However, whenever the first person became aware that there was something or someone greater than him- or herself and other people, that person sought to know more and to form a relationship with the presence of Divine Mystery. When that person started searching, he or she discovered something surprising, as it soon dawned on the seeker that the one he or she was seeking seemed to be returning the favor: the seeker was also being pursued.[1]

The ancestor who might best illustrate "the seeker" is a key man in the three great monotheistic religions that remain active today: Christianity, Judaism, and Islam. In the story of Abraham, faithfully preserved in the Hebrew Scriptures in the Book of Genesis and repeatedly referred to in the Koran, religious seekers are introduced to a Bedouin nomad who desires to respond to the stirrings within him. Contemporary men and women, looking through the mist of history, do not know for certain that Abraham's quest was primarily spiritual, but his story has many of the components that are traditionally considered necessary to engage in such a journey.

According to the Torah and the Koran, and in the oral tradition that supports both holy books, Abraham seems highly motivated to consistently encounter the presence of Divine Mystery and to establish a relationship with God. The Koran informs the reader that, from early childhood, Abraham sensed the presence of the "other," whom he identified as the "one God." Abraham desired to serve only this presence, which he assumed to be divine. In a world where many gods were worshiped and numerous spiritual paths and religious traditions were followed, Abraham remained focused on his pursuit, succeeding in establishing communication with the one God he pursued.

In the Torah, the reader meets Abraham as an old man, where the story becomes dramatic. It is the point when communication between Abraham and the presence of Divine Mystery has been established. This dramatic moment, core to the Jewish and the Christian traditions, is known as the covenant between Yahweh and Abraham, effectively ratifying the relationship for all time: "I will…be your God and the God of your descendants after you" (Genesis 17:7).

Missing from these stories is insight or detail about Abraham's pursuit. The holy books don't inform us of his countless hours of reflection. We have no proof of his wonderings, doubts, and questions, which would be part and parcel of a transition from accepting the gods of polytheism to worshiping the one God of monotheism.

It would not have been easy for Abraham to set aside old habits and religious practices. It would have been equally difficult for him to convince others to do the same. Wives, sons, daughters, and other members of the patriarchal family may not have shared the conviction that had formed deep within Abraham and inspired his search. It would have been necessary for this conviction to eventually manifest itself as belief. Abraham had a strongly held spiritual value that would animate the rest of his life and define his relationships.

In addition, the Old Testament does not reveal a fully formed and spiritually mature ancestor in faith. The Koran comes closer to such a portrayal. The contemporary reader should not expect that Abraham's spiritual and religious formation is fully integrated, because it is a story that speaks only of his first encounter with the presence of Divine Mystery. Abraham is not fully formed or spiritually mature in the way we define such maturity today. He is a product of his time, and we should not expect otherwise. It is enough that the stories from Scripture effectively help people learn valuable lessons from Abraham's quest and life. These stories retain their ability to clearly illustrate some of the requirements for today's spiritual journey.[2]

Abraham was a patriarch who was quite happy with his position. Nothing indicates he was suffering from any kind of angst because of his patriarchal habits and opinions. Abraham's story also suggests that the presence of Divine Mystery (Yahweh), whom Abraham encounters, also exhibits the qualities and sensibilities of a patriarch. Yahweh engages Abraham in the way Abraham is most comfortable: patriarch to patriarch. Abraham the patriarch is looking for something that will prove to be an advantage to his tribe. The presence of Divine Mystery, Yahweh, is also looking for something, but not necessarily anything that will increase his advantage.

The Hebrew Scriptures also do not adequately present the spiritual journey of Sarah, a major and essential participant. Yes, it was a patriarchal society, but it would be foolhardy to believe that Sarah just sat on the sidelines. The story remains largely silent about Abraham's primary wife and keeper of the household. Even so, it is more accurate to affirm that this story is about Abraham and Sarah, not just about the patriarch.

Returning to our story, there is still much to learn. Remember, both Yahweh and Abraham are seekers. Both receive what they seek as a result of an equal patriarchic agreement that we can summarize with: "I will do this, and you will do that, then you will receive this, and I will receive that."

From our position a few thousand years later, we should not be surprised by the simplicity of the exchange found in Scripture. Remember, the story intends to teach us about a relationship, and most relationships begin on this basic level. Indeed, the trust level increases as Yahweh and Abraham relate to one another. Vulnerability becomes possible, even necessary. Then, and only then, does the intimacy between Yahweh and Abraham deepen, growing in richness and complexity. It is not far-fetched to assert that the relationship becomes much freer than it was at the beginning. Maturity deepens relationships.

The lesson from the first encounter between the presence of Divine Mystery and Abraham and Sarah is that Yahweh encounters this first man and woman of fragile faith exactly as they are. We can conclude that Yahweh engages in and enables the relationship from that starting point. The story thus teaches a valuable lesson: a person who desires to enter a relationship with Yahweh does not have to be perfect or fully formed. The journey begins wherever you are. It unfolds from there, with the presence of Divine Mystery with you.

This first relationship between the presence of Divine Mystery and humanity portrays Yahweh as enjoying the process of the relationship and the details and nuances as they take place. Plus, Yahweh is patient with the many detours and false starts that are to be expected as any relationship develops. Other men and women of the sacred testaments have equally dramatic and poignant stories to share with us for helpful reflection.

One biblical character whose relationship with Divine Mystery has captured the imaginations of thousands of generations is King David. Abraham, Sarah, Isaac, Jacob, Rebecca, Joseph, Moses, Joshua, and other men and women all have significant places in the story of and the relationship between Yahweh and the people of the covenant. However wonderful and enriching their relationships were, it is King David who holds a special place in the pages of the Christian Scripture and the Jewish Torah. His story is intimate, tender, and emotional. It encompasses a full range of human emotions, none of which have been papered over by the storytellers but rather exposed for all to reflect upon.

When we first find David in 1 Samuel and 2 Samuel, there is immediate drama. Samuel the prophet has been sent by the Lord to Jesse, a patriarch in Bethlehem. He is the father of eight sons, one of whom is to be chosen and anointed as the king of Israel. Jesse presents his seven oldest sons to Samuel for his consideration, but none of them are of interest to him. But when the youngest son of Jesse—"ruddy, a youth with beautiful eyes, and good looking" (1 Samuel 16:12)—is presented to Samuel, the prophet takes notice.

Samuel hears the voice of the Lord, who identifies the boy, David, as the one who has been called and chosen. From that moment on, David is seized by the "Spirit of Yahweh," and his relationship with the Lord is played out. And what an adventure it is!

King David's is a story that includes a battle with a Philistine goliath of a man, whom David slays in the name of Yahweh. His tale features an intimate friendship with the son of a king, Jonathan, who loves David as "his very self" (1 Samuel 18:3) and who later suffers a tragic death at the side of his father, all while staying loyal and faithful to David. The king has marriages, some for political convenience, one for love, and one—to Bathsheba—for reasons rooted in lust. His marriage to Bathsheba turns out well, though, with the birth of the future King Solomon. Also threaded through David's story are military escapades, plots and coup attempts, murders, and one spectacular display of religious piety and devotion to Yahweh when David, stripped to the bare necessities, dances with joy before the Ark of the Covenant as it is carried into the city of Jerusalem (2 Samuel 6:14–15).

Each adventure makes for a wonderful story, but these stories do not necessarily help us understand why King David is so appealing. For the answer, I think it is important to discuss two standout moments from his life. One reveals dramatic repentance and acceptance of responsibility. The other displays reflection and heartfelt thanksgiving for a long and fruitful life.

David dramatically repents and accepts responsibility for his guilt when the prophet Nathan confronts him. Yahweh sends Nathan to David when the events concerning Uriah, Bathsheba, and the lustful, deceptive, and murderous king come to light. The story is beautifully related in 2 Samuel:

> *[Nathan said to David,] "Tell me how you judge this case: In a certain town there were two men, one rich, the other poor. The rich man had flocks and herds in great numbers. But the poor man had nothing at all except one little ewe lamb that he had bought. He nourished her, and she grew up with him and his children. Of what little he had she ate; from his own cup she drank; in his bosom she slept; she was like a daughter to him. Now, a visitor came to the rich man, but he spared his own flocks and herds to prepare a meal for the traveler who had come to him: he took the poor man's ewe lamb and prepared it for the one who had come to him." David grew very angry with that man and said to Nathan: "As the LORD lives, the man who has done this deserves death! He shall make fourfold restitution for the lamb because he has done this and was unsparing."*

> 2 SAMUEL 12:1–6

Upon hearing Nathan's tale, David flies into a rage, proclaiming the injustice relayed in the story and demanding punishment and restitution. The God-sent prophet then simply confronts David with starkly pointed words: "You are the man!" (2 Samuel 12:7). Even after almost 3,000 years, the tension in the story is still palpable. Readers can almost feel the eyes of everyone in the room turn to the king of Israel and await his reaction.

Confronted by the seer-prophet but even more by the gravity of his sins, David surprises everyone. He admits his guilt and seeks the forgiveness of God. This story would be dramatic no matter the circumstance, but it is even more heartfelt when we realize that the confrontation, David's admission of guilt, and his desire to repent occur at the peak of his power. He could just as easily have given the opposite response, expressing arrogance with no acceptance of personal responsibility. Powerful people do that all the time. David could have diverted attention from himself and shifted blame to another. The fact that David immediately rejects the path of the arrogant and assumes the posture of the vulnerable and the humble is riveting, revealing his true character.[3]

As moving and inspirational as this moment is, the

second character revelation perhaps focuses our attention more sharply. This moment helps us understand David's relationship with Yahweh. It shows why David remains so beloved, despite his significant faults and failings. The event takes place at the end of his life.

In 2 Samuel, David is deep in prayer and thought. He is fully aware that his days on earth are ending. As a powerful king, he might be understandably distracted by his impending death. He is certainly experiencing the struggles that come with the succession of power to his anointed son, as well as any of a multitude of other issues. Such diversions may well occupy some of his time, but he is more focused on his relationship with the Lord. He prays the prayer of a man who is completely aware of the power of God and the favor that God has repeatedly shown to him.

O LORD, my rock, my fortress, my deliverer,
my God, my rock of refuge!
My shield, my saving horn,
my stronghold, my refuge,
my savior, from violence you keep me safe.
Praised be the LORD, I exclaim!
I have been delivered from my enemies.

2 SAMUEL 22:2–4

While Abraham and Sarah's story teaches spiritual seekers about the kind of persistence that can be required in seeking a relationship with Divine Mystery, King David's tale illustrates another equally important concept. David's relationship with Yahweh is full of important bumps and detours on the spiritual path. The only constant factor for David in the relationship is the depth of emotion he feels for Yahweh. King David often forgets or misplaces the actions and the choices of a spiritually mature and morally upright person. However, despite his less-than-vigilant attention to the details of his essential relationship with Yahweh, we see a profound depth in their connection, which is often strained but never broken. King David loves Yahweh, and Yahweh loves David.

The Judeo-Christian ancestors in faith are not limited to the people of the testaments who dominate the pages of the sacred Scriptures. Although the patriarch, Abraham; his wife, Sarah; and King David offer formidable examples, many other people of faith have connected to the experience of the presence of Divine Mystery. These people are unnamed and not regularly celebrated, but they made major contributions to humanity's understanding of this relationship and spiritual connection. When we remember their journey of faith in response to the call they heard, we also might experience an encounter with the presence of Divine Mystery.[4]

Ancestors in Faith—New Testament

In the New Testament of the Christian Scriptures, you will find many stories of individual and communal encounters with the presence of Divine Mystery. One person's relationship with the manifestation of the Divine Presence, in this instance with the Incarnate Son of God in the person of Jesus, is the woman from Galilee known as Mary of Magdala or Mary Magdalene.[5] Mary's characterization in the New Testament is not necessarily dramatic or extensive, at least at first reading. However, upon further reflection and from a certain Christian interpretative perspective, perhaps it is more dramatic than it might originally appear.

We're introduced to Mary Magdalene in the fifteenth chapter of the Gospel of Mark, which was the first gospel written. In Mark 15, Mary Magdalene is standing at the foot of the cross of the crucified Jesus.[6] Here, we learn she was part of a group of women who had ministered to Jesus many times and had provided hospitality to him throughout his life as an itinerant preacher. Her presence at this moment of his greatest agony, and the presence of the other women at the foot of the cross, stands in stark contrast to the absence of most of the male apostles and disciples, who had evidently fled the scene of this horror.

We next encounter Mary Magdalene a little later in Mark's Gospel, and this is substantially confirmed in the later editions of the gospels, those of Matthew and Luke. In each version, early in the morning, on "the first day of the week," Mary Magdalene is on her way to the burial place of Jesus, intent on preparing his body for a more proper burial. Upon her arrival at the temporary place of his entombment, she finds that it was much more temporary than anyone might have imagined. Jesus is not in the tomb, and his body is no longer present. The Gospel of John presents the story in this manner:

> *But Mary stayed outside the tomb weeping. And as she wept, she bent over into the tomb and saw two angels in white sitting there, one at the head and one at the feet where the body of Jesus had been. And they said to her, "Woman, why*

are you weeping?" She said to them, "They have taken my Lord, and I don't know where they laid him." When she had said this, she turned around and saw Jesus there, but did not know it was Jesus. Jesus said to her, "Woman, why are you weeping? Whom are you looking for?" She thought it was the gardener and said to him, "Sir, if you carried him away, tell me where you laid him, and I will take him." Jesus said to her, "Mary!" She turned and said to him in Hebrew, "Rabbouni," which means Teacher. Jesus said to her, "Stop holding on to me, for I have not yet ascended to the Father. But go to my brothers and tell them, 'I am going to my Father and your Father, to my God and your God.'" Mary of Magdala went and announced to the disciples, "I have seen the Lord," and what he told her.

JOHN 20:11–18 [7]

Two essential components of the spiritual encounter and journey are made explicitly clear. First, Mary Magdalene is called by name. She responds immediately with unequivocal belief and commitment, followed by action. Second, she is sent to the other apostles and the disciples with her dramatic testimony that Jesus has been raised from the dead. Being called and sent are essential points of connection with Divine Mystery. She was the first evangelizer, the first witness of the Christian life.

Moreover, it is essential in her story and in other stories that might be referenced that Mary's response to being called and sent represents an authentic and personal experience. The authenticity is compelling and necessary. The response is not a kind of report of a collective memory, the response of some other person, or a retelling of someone else's story. It is not a religious response; it is a spiritual experience. Mary was a personal and authentic witness to what she experienced as well as how she understood and interpreted that experience when she shared it.

When contrasting the King David and Mary Magdalene stories, I invite you to consider an enriching interpretation. David's response to the presence of Divine Mystery can be seen, in one sense, as a complicated love story played out on a public stage. Mary Magdalene's is also a love story, but it seems to be neither convoluted nor complicated. Mary seems to love fully, giving herself entirely over to profound intimacy and attachment.

Perhaps the further maturing of her relationship with Jesus comes with her experience and personal lifelong witness to the power of resurrection. As her relationship deepens, she will be slowly invited and enabled by the power of grace to see Jesus not only as teacher but also as Lord.

Mary Magdalene represents those who knew and lived with and near the historical Jesus. This group is representative of a particular historical time and place. The group and its setting cannot be duplicated, and their numbers cannot be increased. Another reality is expressed in the stories of the people who became Christians right after the resurrection and the ascension. They are close to the historical moment but outside it, and so their experience is not the same. Perhaps the most complex spiritual story of what became a Christian encounter with Divine Mystery is the story of Paul of Tarsus.

I have always been intrigued by Paul, especially the enthusiasm and obvious excitement he feels for his mission and ministry in the name of the risen Christ. I have often wondered how he could have become so dedicated to his mission of evangelization without ever experiencing a personal relationship with the historical Jesus.

His was seemingly a mystical encounter, one further shrouded in what seems to be, at the core, a life-changing vision of the risen Christ. His experience also pulled him away from a highly disciplined and defined religious practice into a completely different one. It is a powerful yet flabbergasting story. I am sure that many of Paul's contemporaries were dumbfounded and confused by what happened. No one could have predicted it.

One interpretation of Paul's encounter with the presence of Divine Mystery is that it was not primarily relational or dependent on a personal experience of the person of Jesus. It was not played out in an arena that includes growth in trust, a deepening vulnerability, and then some experience of intimacy. Rather, it seems that the encounter was played out in the realm of ideas about the risen Christ, the role of the law, the power of grace, and many other thoughts. Because of these insights—which Paul expressed—Paul often clashed with people who knew and remembered the Jesus who had walked the earth and who came to believe through their personal relationships with him. They could not remember anything in their experiences with or related to the Jesus they knew that came close to what Paul was expressing about Jesus.

The torrent of ideas and descriptions, and the theological basis of the Christian faith that has been handed down, reveals that Paul's encounter and experience were powerful beyond comprehension and words—so powerful, in fact, that they contradicted his previous beliefs of what he had learned to be necessary for salvation. He struggles to describe and define what he knows to be essential and true about the risen Christ. His struggle is important, illustrative of a reality perfectly summarized in the Gospel of John: "Blessed are those who have not seen and have believed" (John 20:29).

For those who desire to believe as a Christian, Paul's story is important and inspiring. While he had no in-person relationship with the historical Jesus, Paul nonetheless develops a deep faith and spiritual practice—and more. His relationship moved from a religious experience to the spiritual and then to an integration of both. How else can one explain the depth of feeling and intimacy that is so often expressed in his writings?

Love is patient, love is kind. It is not jealous, [love] is not pompous, it is not inflated, it is not rude, it does not seek its own interests, it is not quick-tempered, it does not brood over injury, it does not rejoice over wrongdoing but rejoices with the truth. It bears all things, believes all things, hopes all things, endures all things. Love never fails. If there are prophecies, they will be brought to nothing; if tongues, they will cease; if knowledge, it will be brought to nothing.

1 CORINTHIANS 13:4–8

The Wisdom of Jesus

Jesus was born into a culture that was steeped in an individual and a communitarian belief in God. His parents, reflecting their deep roots of this belief, named him *Yeshua*, meaning "Yahweh saves." Jesus, his parents, and their extended family were people who identified with the story of Abraham. The collective words of the prophets were not the voices of history but the voices of God's truth—the promises to be fulfilled to those who remained faithful to the covenant. Jesus' family enthusiastically shared the stories of the great King David, believing that what once was would one day be reality for them. And, perhaps most important, they lived in anticipation of the imminent, sudden, and unannounced manifestation of the power of God from his place of residence in the heavens.

The prophetic message, preached to the people of Jesus' time and place for more than 1,000 years, was one that reminded them of their sinfulness but primarily reminded them of God's desire to be with his people and to make things right. As a people who lived in an occupied land and who were oppressed in their poverty, they longed for the day when God's people, the little ones, would be restored to their proper place of respect and dignity. Until that day, however, they needed to scrape together a living and find a way to survive. That was their reality, and the penalties were harsh and immediate for anyone who might forget this truth.

For the first thirty years of his life, before his baptism in the Jordan River by John the Baptist, Jesus lived in the backwater town of Nazareth. It was an extremely poor village, as recent archeological excavations of the site have confirmed. It was the home to day laborers who perhaps found work in the not-too-distant city of Sepphoris. That bustling city was experiencing the trickle-down effects of the lavish patronage of King Herod, whose intent was to rebuild the city and return it to a place of prominence.

The proposed building-up of Sepphoris was not

guaranteed. Just a few years before the birth of Jesus, Sepphoris had been destroyed. The city had been razed to the ground by Roman occupiers in response to its perceived treason and rebellion during a short period of unrest. But by AD 6, Sepphoris was the focus of renewed and frenzied activity. The days of rebellion and destruction were faint memories, replaced by a new reality. Opportunity was the name of the game. There was an obvious and pronounced need not only for skilled artisans but also for the unskilled laborers who could support their effort, according to the book *Excavating Jesus: Beneath the Stones, Behind the Texts*. Nazareth, by contrast, was not great and never would be. It was just a place to live, to lay one's weary head, to dream of something better.

While lacking grandeur, Nazareth was an ideal spot for establishing and deepening a relationship with the presence of Divine Mystery. There were no significant distractions. The Temple, with its scribes and Pharisees, was far away. In Nazareth, people had a routine of daily life, and silence and solitude were easily within reach. For Jesus, a sensitive boy with a keen ability to perceive and understand life, his little town was also home to the mysterious and the sacred. For those who wanted a deep relationship with the presence of Divine Mystery, Nazareth was where they might encounter the "burning bush" of the great ancestor Moses. It was holy ground (see Exodus 3).

Some thirty years after his birth, Jesus emerged from Nazareth and began his life of public ministry. Not only was he a man now, but he had often experienced the burn of the presence of Divine Mystery. Jesus proclaimed his personal relationship with this presence, not with the tired words and concepts of the scribes and the Pharisees, but rather with real stories of encounter and experience. For Jesus, the presence of Divine Mystery was Abba, the Father with whom a trusting, vulnerable, and authentically intimate relationship was both possible and desired.

As his ministry unfolded, Jesus decided not to debate with the representatives of the temple cult in Jerusalem, who may well have had different ideas of God. He and his growing number of followers witnessed the power of an authentic spiritual experience and contrasted it with the old-time religious discipline that seemed lifeless—or, if not lifeless, certainly demanding and exhausting.

Jesus shared with his hearers his experience of Abba. In his deliberate and telling contrast to other teachers, Jesus shared his conviction that Abba was not far away from them but rather very close. His preaching and teaching excited the people of Galilee. His passionate message invited them to imagine and hope that the presence of Divine Mystery had not abandoned them. Jesus assured his listeners that Abba was intimately and passionately concerned for them. Abba God, Jesus said, loved the people and had compassion for them all the time.[8]

Contextual Commentary

Your spiritual quest probably did not begin on a windswept plain with animal herds and family surrounding you, as it did for Abraham and Sarah. There's no need to compare your story to the tales of King David or the intimacy felt by Mary Magdalene. However, your quest and that of everyone else is just as significant and essential, and the twenty-first century presents its own challenges to welcoming the "other" into our lives. With a myriad of distractions, voices, images, and potential choices, the single most difficult challenge might be to identify the stirrings, the "call" to the spiritual.[9]

Experience suggests that some might even identify this call and invitation as something else, in the sincere belief that they have correctly realized what is churning the spirit within them. As a result, instead of recognizing the stirring within as a spiritual moment and embarking on a spiritual quest, a person might turn to a different job or seek to change his or her primary relationships, believing they are stale and no longer life-giving. Others may turn to therapy, a new exercise program, or the latest diet. Many people might never even consider the possibility that what is going on within them could be the ancient call of the presence of Divine Mystery, who still seeks to establish and develop relationships.

When people get tired of old ways of thinking, when the distractions that once succeeded in getting them through the day no longer seem to work, when they feel lifeless or uninspired, or when they start to wonder "what it's all about," they may be responding to an ancient stirring within that is calling them to engage with life in a different way. When a person listens to another person and nods in agreement, all the while believing there is something more—the "yes, but" of life—that person may be experiencing a call to deepening spiritual growth and development. If this restlessness is from the Holy One, if it is truly a spiritual call and invitation, it will not go away. Each man and woman who hears this call is required to respond to it in some way.

The feeling that there is something more to life, which propelled Abraham and Sarah, King David, and Mary Magdalene, is the spark of the spiritual journey. When people respond, they take the first step on a path to the Holy One, God, the Sacred—however they refer to and see the presence of Divine Mystery.

However a person comes to engage with the spiritual call, he or she is embarking on a wonderful journey that will lead to the fullness of health, wholeness, and holiness. It is a journey that many people, from many different faith traditions, connect with in response to a call or perhaps some kind of restlessness. These people will join their steps together and will discover and learn to appreciate the power and grace of the Holy One. The spiritual journey is a lifelong and eternal quest.

Although you may be newly aware of the presence of Divine Mystery as you start on your spiritual journey, the decision to take the first step is personal. It is an initial connection in response to the grace of God; a call to begin the process of growing toward spiritual maturity. Those who answer this call will not be the same at the end of their journey. Every part of daily living—the good and the bad, the brilliant and the challenging—has the potential to form them into the fully alive and engaged people that the presence of Divine Mystery invites us to be.

Disconnect

People who have connected with the presence of Divine Mystery and find this connection important typically believe that it will animate and energize their perceptions and judgments about the meaning of life. As Christians, and particularly as Catholics, this belief informs our basic understanding of spirituality and relationship with God, whom we call Abba, Father.

We may assume that a lifelong relationship with God, however we know God, is a position that most people share with other Christians.[10] However, that assumption may no longer be valid. People are increasingly aware that they live in a world in which they encounter long-lived spiritual traditions and practices that do not mirror traditional Christian theology. Many spiritual perspectives today do not acknowledge the existence of a personal God who wants individual and communal relationships with people.

In addition to the presence of other spiritual traditions, there is a growing awareness that some men and women, once assumed to be people of the Christian tradition but who no longer follow the tradition, are quite satisfied to reject Christian revelation. Social scientists and other professionals who study the constructs of modern culture and society have identified a growing number of people who identify themselves as agnostic, meaning they are skeptical about the existence of God.[14] Others are atheists who have no interest in connecting with spiritual traditions and are committed to ignoring or disconnecting from them.

Although the *Catechism of the Catholic Church* acknowledges these realities, it is unsympathetic toward them: "But this 'intimate and vital bond of man to God' can be forgotten, overlooked, or even explicitly rejected by man. Such attitudes can have different causes: revolt against evil in the world; religious ignorance or indifference; the cares and riches of the world; the scandal of bad example on the part of believers; currents of thought hostile to religion; finally, that attitude of sinful man which makes him hide from God out of fear and flee his call" (*CCC* 29).

As men and women of faith who seek to have an honest, authentic, and mature spiritual practice, it's important for us to follow the *Catechism* and acknowledge the changing circumstances of this time and place. The presence of other spiritual traditions and practices, including the "nones" (people with no religious or spiritual convictions), does not interfere with anyone else's spiritual and faith journey. Let the nones be. You can follow your own path.

The COVID-19 pandemic forever changed many patterns and practices that people had seen as normal. The required isolation became the norm and stayed that way long after the need for it ended. The pandemic accelerated a movement that had been developing slowly. It did not create an exodus, but it enabled it.

Many people stopped going to church. Organized religion and religious events were simply too much of a risk to be encouraged, so people stayed home. Sundays passed, and there were no gatherings. The skies did not open; thunder and lightning did not strike; there was rather an almost deafening silence. A new reality was being claimed, tragically: *It is not necessary to be part of a religious discipline; spiritual practice seems to be nourishment enough.* When church congregations could gather again, the pews did not fill up.

Why are churches emptier now? It will be researched

and studied for years to come. This might be a little too simplistic, but perhaps the people in the pews were simply not nourished. When the going-to-church habit was broken, former churchgoers saw no reason to return. There was no real hunger, no sense of being well fed. Frankly, people did not feel starved or in any way deprived when their ability to attend church was disrupted. It is easy to change a pattern or to walk a different path when you are abandoning an experience that feels lifeless.

Here is a perspective that may or may not be true: For the now-absent people who used to go to church, perhaps there was way too much religion and not enough spiritual experience. No authentic religious experience, no relationship with people or the presence of Divine Mystery, only a system and the institution that represented it. That system was disconnected from most aspects of everyday life, resulting in no compelling reason for many people to show up and worship. So, they didn't.

Chapter One Notes

1. *The Essential Catholic Handbook*, a Redemptorist Pastoral Publication, defines dogmatic teaching as "A teaching or doctrine authoritatively and explicitly proposed by the Church as revealed by God and requiring the belief of the people of God."

2. "I believe in God" (*CCC* 199). This first affirmation of the Apostles' Creed is also the most fundamental.

3. Elizabeth A. Johnson, CSJ, writes in *Quest for the Living God: Mapping Frontiers in the Theology of God*, "A Zen-like riddle preached by Augustine preserves this wisdom succinctly: 'If you have understood, it is not God' (Sermon 117.5). If you have fully figured out who God is, then you are dealing with something else, some lesser reality. It is a matter of the livingness of God, who is not just a bigger and better object in the world but the unspeakably Other."

4. St. Alphonsus Liguori (1696–1787), a doctor of the Catholic Church and spiritual teacher, wrote that "we desire because first we have been desired." Saint Alphonsus believed, as do many other spiritual teachers, that there is within people an innate call, an invitation, or perhaps just a stirring that orients people toward spiritual wholeness and unity. We respond to this part of ourselves at different times for many different reasons.

5. I am convinced of the authenticity of the encounter between Abraham (and Sarah) and the presence of Divine Mystery. My conviction does not rest on the details of the story as it has been preserved but rather on a particular theme that is part and par-

cel of this encounter as well as an essential component of the stories that follow it. The writers of Genesis were steeped in the tradition that identified men and women as people "formed in the image and likeness of God." In the story of Abraham, it seems that humanity is all too willing to return the favor and form the presence of Divine Mystery in the image and likeness of man. Divine Mystery's resistance to this constricting complement is pivotal. The presence of Divine Mystery's self-identification as "I Am Who I Am," leads me to believe that the encounter was genuine, even if it was not fully appreciated by the representatives of the person.

6. Recall this story when we examine the fourth connecting point. Here, David shows that the spiritual connecting points can occur throughout life and are not dependent on our ability to perfect any one experience. However, the more we are aware of a point of connection, the more we can learn and then respond to the invitation to develop spiritual maturity.

7. Pope Francis writes in *Evangelii Gaudium*, "The believer is essentially one who remembers" (*EG* 13).

8. Susan Haskins writes in *Mary Magdalen: Myth and Metaphor* that Magdala, or el Mejdel, was a prosperous fishing village on the northwest bank of Lake Galilee, and the town was destroyed around the year 75. The people of el Mejdel had a reputation for licentious behavior and living, which may well explain the identification of Mary as a sinner or, even worse, a prostitute.

9. While Mary Magdalene appears slightly earlier in the gospel account by the evangelist Luke (Chapter 8), scholars agree that Mark was the earliest gospel written.

10. See also Mark 16:1–8, Matthew 28:1–8, and Luke 24:1–12. All gospel texts probably draw on Mark, although John's version, which speaks so clearly of the appearance of Mary Magdalene, may be from an unknown, independent source.

11. I have discovered many wonderful, useful books on coming to an understanding and appreciation of who Jesus is and how he might have lived. I am particularly impressed with José Antonio Pagola's *Jesus: An Historical Approximation* (Convivium Press, 2009). I highly recommend it.

12. Elizabeth A. Johnson, CSJ, also writes in *Quest for the Living God*, "Furthermore, when a person does come to engage belief in a personal way, society makes this difficult to do. For modern society is marked not only by atheism and agnosticism but also by positivism, which restricts what we can know to data accessible from the natural sciences; secularism, which gets on with the business at hand, impatient of ultimate questions, with a wealth of humanistic values that allow a life of ethical integrity without faith; and religious pluralism, which demonstrates that there is more than one path to holy and ethical living."

13. Many commentators on the spiritual life agree that there are at least three distinct components, three distinct realities, that come into consideration: capacity (the choice to integrate and encounter experience), style/type (the way we relate to the sense of the sacred and the world in which we live), and discipline (the focus of the capacity to be spiritual within a particular expression of spirituality). A particularly useful resource to continue this study is Bradley R. Holt's *Thirsty for God: A Brief History of Christian Spirituality* (Fortress Press, 2005).

14. From World Pantheism Movement (pantheism.net): "You might be uncertain whether the God of your culture's main religion, or any god, exists; You might be a principled agnostic who believes that the question of God's existence is unanswerable, that proof either way is impossible; You might be a practical agnostic and believe that the question of God's existence is irrelevant to the living of life."

CHAPTER TWO

Discipline and Practice

Learning to Focus Attention

"The unaware life is a mechanical life. It's not human, it's programmed, conditioned. We might as well be a stone, a block of wood."

ANTHONY DE MELLO, SJ, *AWARENESS*

"When we sit, we know we are sitting. When we walk, we know we are walking. When we eat, we know we are eating."

THICH NHAT HANH, QUOTING THE BUDDHA

"When one's thoughts are neither frivolous nor flippant; when one's thoughts are neither stiff-necked nor stupid, but rather are harmonious—they habitually render physical calm and deep insight."

HILDEGARD OF BINGEN, *MEDITATIONS WITH HILDEGARD OF BINGEN*

"This is why you must now acknowledge, and fix in your heart, that the LORD is God in the heavens above and on earth below, and that there is no other. And you must keep his statutes and commandments which I command you today, that you and your children after you may prosper, and that you may have long life on the land which the LORD, your God, is giving you forever."

DEUTERONOMY 4:39–40

Building a Disciplined Spiritual Practice

The writings of Thomas Merton (1915–1968), a Trappist monk and mystic, are referred to often by people of many different faiths and traditions. In his book *The Holy Longing*, Ronald Rolheiser, OMI, presents one of Merton's observations that we can apply in the present tense: "One of the most critical spiritual challenges is efficiency. We are too focused on work and too pragmatic, spending all our time keeping the factory and the business running, leaving little time and energy for anything else."

Merton's use of the term "efficiency" probably reflects the historical situation of his time. Efficiency was considered a great value, something to be attained and praised. When Merton observed that people were too efficient, it was a commentary on misplaced focus and energy. Today, the word that might best describe our problem is "scattered."

Too many demands are placed on our time, but we need to meet every demand so we can make ends meet. Demands include our time working and commuting, raising a family, and sustaining a relationship. It all seems never-ending. Maintaining a household and the other routine tasks that consume our time often bring men and women to a point of exhaustion at the end of the day. Once people arrive home after the workday, their bodies are tired, their minds are stretched to the point where it is impossible to concentrate and reflect, and their spirits are often drained.

People in this state of mind and spirit want nothing more than some kind of relief. They want something that will relax them, distract them, and fill in the few hours before it is time for bed, and then they start the entire routine all over again.

As if the daily grind is not challenging enough, fear also becomes part of their lives, as indirectly referenced by Merton. This fear is the feeling of anxiety and unrest that results from slowing down, taking a breath, and changing the scenery for any length of time. This fear is present not because people don't yearn for a break; the fear exists because of the belief—which is not baseless—that if they choose to take time off, their careers might be adversely affected.

For example, someone may fear missing a business meeting, thinking that his or her employer might perceive him or her as not dedicated enough or not truly committed to success. For this reason, even during time away from the workplace, many people continue checking and responding to emails and voicemail messages to keep up with the latest developments.

This experience of life, sometimes called the "rat race," is all too common; it is often a typical rather than extraordinary circumstance—so it should come as no surprise to anyone that these fears and perceptions seem normal or even expected. Moreover, it's also not surprising that this type of experience is found in other areas of life, not just in the workplace.

For example, some churches—where religious expression and worship is supposed to take place—have in many instances become mirror images of the culture. Instead of traditional places of silence, prayer, and reflection, some communities of worship have become another kind of distraction.

These churches are advertised as places of fellowship. They often feature performing choirs and energetic, animated, and even entertaining preaching. The services are presented in a slick, fast-paced style, intended to get the congregation "in and out" within a certain time limit. When people walk out the door, their spirits have hopefully been lifted, and—as is often the case—their wallets are probably a bit lighter.

It is quite possible to attend a church service in such a

setting and never experience one prolonged moment of silence or inactivity. The church, instead of being an oasis from the stress of living—a place where worshipers can clearly identify, cultivate, and reverence the most important things in life—contributes to the overall feeling of being disconnected and out of touch. People may not even be sure what they experience at this type of church. Is it worship? Entertainment? A pep rally?

People may feel immediate satisfaction after such a church service; they at least have the satisfaction of knowing that they've responded to some part of their spiritual and religious personhood. However, the feeling is fleeting. This instant satisfaction is not sustainable and often wears off quickly—maybe by the time the congregation reaches their cars in the crowded parking lot.

And it is not just attendance at a "mega-church" that can be distracting and lacking in spiritual nourishment. A lackluster and poorly planned liturgical ritual, with lifeless preaching, unenthusiastic participation, and the overwhelming feeling of fulfilling an obligation, elicits the same result. It is not sustainable and makes no real difference in life. Such an encounter also contributes to the conclusion that the experience is disconnected from authenticity and from what people really need.

More and more people, because of the crush of life and because they perceive little potential engagement with the presence of Divine Mystery, have learned to mistrust silence, inactivity, and solitude. They reject mediocrity and are unwilling to settle for simply fulfilling an obligation or meeting expectations that have been placed upon them by others.

In effect, they have learned to mistrust those moments in their lives when there is seemingly nothing going on. Instead of feeding the spirit that needs nourishment, they allow their hunger to become even more pronounced. When someone hungers for something of substance in life, and this need is unfulfilled, the person will fill this void with something—anything—that distracts him or her.

The ultimate distraction that readily fills the void is what Merton stated: efficiency, or misplaced attention—people's tendency to always need to be doing something rather than nothing. In our fast-paced society, it seems there must always be background noise or images flashing in front of our eyes, or we become uncomfortable. We mistrust inactivity, as illustrated by these common examples.

First, observe the behavior of some people in their

cars as they wait for a traffic light to change, especially if a red light lasts a little longer than they expected. Notice how quickly some people get impatient and angry over waiting for the light to change; road rage is one extreme outcome. Second, observe people in line at the grocery store or anywhere else, especially if the line is not moving fast enough for them. Notice how quickly they try to fill the time by doing something on their phone, picking up a magazine from the display rack, or even rearranging the food in their cart. Many find it almost impossible to just stand patiently and wait their turn.

Spiritual masters of most disciplines and all kinds of faith traditions insist that an important and crucial step in the spiritual journey is to become focused on living. Life is not just something that happens; it is intended to be enjoyed, experienced fully. Life is the pathway to integrity and wholeness, which is what we might identify as becoming spiritual.

To grow in awareness of how we live our lives, we must learn not to avoid inactivity but to seek it out. Again, referencing the spiritual traditions and the established disciplines of spiritual growth, the master gently, and sometimes not so gently, prods his or her students to become mindful of the choices and the decisions that they make each day. Spiritual masters and teachers invite students to try and become aware of all that is going on at any given moment. This exercise helps people focus their attention and comprehend how difficult it is to become comfortable with doing so.

To concretely demonstrate this point and teach its necessity, a spiritual master will assign his or her students a simple challenge. Its purpose is to illustrate how difficult it can be for people to consistently focus their attention and become fully aware of what is happening around them, and the students are not told what the point of the exercise is.

One example of such a mindfulness challenge is for people to try and fully taste, smell, and enjoy food or drink. The teacher gives the students instructions but does not reveal the point of the exercise. Students are first directed to choose something they enjoy eating or drinking—the simpler, the better. They are then directed to sit down with the beverage or food and try to focus their attention on what they are consuming. The spiritual master encourages them to spend a couple of minutes simply enjoying what they are doing, knowing full well that the students will be resisting the temptation to think about what the task is supposed to teach them. Only after they have spent a few precious moments enjoying their food or drink are they encouraged to begin reflecting on what they just did.

The spiritual master will direct the students to identify their perceptions and judgments about what they just experienced, guiding them questions such as, "Was attempting to focus your attention difficult or easy for you?" or "Were you surprised at how quickly or slowly the time passed during this activity?" Each of the students' answers will provide them with a beginning insight into what spiritual masters may generally define as "growing in awareness."

Further reflection, based on a non-Judeo-Christian spiritual tradition, can help deepen an individual's appreciation of the spiritual lesson that can be learned from this exercise. For example, Thich Nhat Hanh, writing about the Buddhist tradition of the Five Contemplations (reflections done before eating) in his book *Living Buddha, Living Christ*, says that focusing attention on a word, such as "mindfulness," may be helpful. The mindfulness exercise, one of many within the spiritual tradition that Hanh represents, is commonly practiced, at least when first introduced by the teacher, at every mealtime gathering with a family or community. A simple review of the words in the following version of the Five Contemplations illustrates the power of this spiritual exercise:

1. This food is the gift of the whole universe, the earth, the sky, and much hard work.
2. May we live in a way that is worthy of the food.
3. May we transform our unskillful states of mind, especially that of greed, and learn to eat with moderation.
4. May we eat only foods that nourish us and prevent illness.
5. May we accept this food for the realization of the way of understanding and love.

Practicing the Five Contemplations results in the focused attention of both the individual and the community who recites the mantra. They consciously engage in consuming the meal that has been prepared and served at a slower, more deliberate pace. The disciplined mindfulness that can result from the choice to be fully aware and mindful of what you are doing is the precious gift of this exercise. Each component of the exercise contributes to your understanding and appreciation of a valuable spiritual lesson.

This kind of spiritual practice, when it is engaged and reflected upon, brings people face to face with a significant truth—a working conviction—that seems to be at the core of many spiritual traditions. This essential truth, although it may seem obvious in retrospect, is often difficult to grasp in the beginning stages of the practice and discipline that focuses one's attention.

Many people, so it has been often observed, spend much of their time worried about the past or anticipating the future. It is the exception to encounter people who choose to deliberately live in the present moment, fully aware of what they are doing at any given moment. This nonjudgmental observation leads to not-at-all-surprising conclusions. By resisting the invitation to live in the present moment and be open to the "now," people unfortunately devote a tremendous amount of energy to maintaining a distracted and unfocused lifestyle,[1] while being unaware of the permanent damage they are causing to the human spirit.

People in developed societies have become accustomed to the expenditure of misplaced energy and assume that it is normal. Even more unsettling is that the culture—dominated by materialism, individualism, and consumerism—thrives on lifestyles of distraction[2] and resists most attempts to focus a person's attention on any specific event or experience. The busy culture leaves little time for reflection or meditation, and it becomes anxious when confronted by people who strive to live contrary to the norm.

People have become consumers not only of every conceivable new product and device but also—perhaps even more so—of events, experiences, choices, and decisions. In the fast-paced rhythm of daily life, it is not unusual for a person to frantically consume the moment-to-moment of everyday life, seemingly unaware of the sheer volume of activity. In such a scenario, a person seldom or never pauses to reflect and discern the meaning of his or her experiences. As a result, the person can become an unfortunate example of distraction. He or she is fully engaged in consumption, with little awareness of what is occurring and even less awareness of the potential cost and consequences.

A necessary connecting point on the spiritual journey, in and of itself a significant sign of spiritual maturity and a deepening contemplative practice, is for the person to learn to resist the driving force of distraction.

To choose, in contrast with the prevailing cultural preferences, to become aware of life and to deliberately take the necessary steps to focus one's individual attention on whatever one is experiencing at any given moment of the day.

A major component of learning and practicing resistance to distraction and becoming more contemplative in life is recognizing that each person can choose to practice awareness/mindfulness. This choice becomes a deliberate and focused practice, posture, and perception of life. As a result, one's attention is heightened and focused on everyday events, from the most important to the banal.

Imagine if the scenario of distracted living were reversed. Imagine a life engaged and lived not in nonstop consumption but in focus, gratitude, and more openness to the mystery and the gifts of life. Imagine, for example, if the words of the Five Contemplations were centered on life instead of on food:

1. My life is a precious gift of the whole universe, the earth, the sky, and the generosity and sacrifice of countless others.

2. May I live this day in a manner that is worthy of the gift that I have been given.

3. May my mind become transformed from an unskillful state, especially that of greed, so I learn to live in moderation.

4. May I only consume those experiences of this precious life that nourish me and the entire human family.

5. May I accept this gift of life, the gift of this moment, for the deepening realization of the way of understanding and love.

A not-uncommon initial reaction when a person first hears the invitation to live a more focused, practiced, and disciplined life is to assume that it is some sort of "crazy talk" and therefore ignore it. A more classical opinion is recorded in Scripture as one of the reactions of certain Greeks, who told the Apostle Paul with some amusement, "We should like to hear you on this some other time" (Acts 17:32). The temptation might be to dismiss the notion right away or to categorize it as something that only a few people can achieve. Some might refer the suggestion to the arena of popularized hype, while still others might label it as New Age, anti-Christian, or "so much hocus-pocus."

It is understandable that this might be some people's first reaction. However, when the spiritual masters talk about growing in awareness and engaging the spiritual practice of learning how to focus individual attention, they are not talking about "navel gazing." They are not talking about becoming self-centered and absorbed. They are not talking about any change in a person's behavior that will be immediately noticeable, except, of course, to the person. What they are trying to teach, what they are trying to invite a person to incorporate into his or her day-to-day living, requires a certain maturity that demands practice, commitment, and resolve—not in and of itself as a specific goal, but as a singular connecting point that leads a person to a deeper and fuller reality.

Focused attention. Awareness. Mindfulness. It does not matter how the practice is identified; all these terms refer to becoming a disciplined person and choosing not to let life just unfold day by day in a never-ending stream. Such a practice indicates that you intend to fully participate in life as it happens. That means you are committed to actively participating in life or, if you prefer a spiritual term, to embracing the revelation of your life as a sacred, meaningful gift.

Awareness means coming to a place of openness, a place of unlimited potential to begin learning to perceive the integral nature of all things, events, and experiences. Mindfulness, as previously noted, is focused attention that encourages a person to practice, commit, and resolve to live in the present moment as much as possible. People choose to live life with focused attention, not for its own sake but as a first step in the lifelong journey of becoming whole, healthy, holy, and spiritually mature. In many spiritual and religious traditions, this step is recognized as a response to the invitation of the presence of Divine Mystery. In the Christian tradition, it is seen as cooperating with the grace offered to each person by God.

It might be difficult for us to recognize the truth and admit that we live undisciplined lives. Often, when people reflect on their lives, they are reluctant to acknowledge this reality. Initially, most people would assert that those who live truly undisciplined lives are incapable of holding down jobs, are criminals, or have life-threatening problems with substance abuse and addiction. It would be rare for someone to willingly accept his or her own life being described as undisciplined.

People find a certain assurance when they cling to

a less-than-truthful perception that they are not like other people, family, friends, and neighbors who have "issues." For this reason, it is difficult for some to acknowledge that they might be undisciplined. One person's problems might not be as noticeable or as destructive as another's. But problems, no matter their severity, can deprive people of health and wholeness.

Most people are eager to acknowledge that certain behaviors and substances are truly harmful. Contemporary culture has adopted a perspective in which most people generally agree about habits that should be avoided, such as drunkenness, drug addiction, smoking, and compulsive eating or shopping.

People who are educated and informed about these matters are at least capable of recognizing the potential harm and danger these habits can cause to their personal health and well-being. People may also recognize unhealthy habits in others and feel that they should be made aware of their destructive behavior. For example, a person with an addiction needs to adopt a recovery program that breaks the habit and leads to sobriety and wellness.

At the same time, other habits are commonly acknowledged as "borderline acceptable," but they can achieve the same kind of harm. Examples include drinking not to the point of drunkenness but to the cusp of drunkenness; watching television or window shopping excessively "just for something to do;" munching on junk food without paying attention to what or how much you are consuming; and clinging to judgmental perceptions and opinions without considering their effect on other people. Just like the previously mentioned destructive habits, these "borderline" behaviors are also truly destructive—possibly to people's physical lives, and most certainly to their spiritual lives. Any habit that can distract, numb, and dull a person's awareness is where the real difficulty lies.

Leading a disciplined life. Leading a life of awareness and focused attention. Adopting the practice of mindfulness. Choosing to live in the present moment. Each discipline contributes to the formation of a spiritual practice that enables a person to walk the path of health and wellness. In some religious traditions, this is the basic definition of a life of holiness.

As your practice develops, you will have to abandon or root out of your life those behaviors you recognize as destructive. This will happen when you connect with more sacred activities and learn to desire no other kind.

You don't necessarily have to change all your habits, but to live a disciplined life, you must at least be aware of what you are choosing, what you are doing, what you are believing.

A disciplined life invites you to seriously consider the reasoning that supports your choosing, doing, and believing. As this new way of engaging in life becomes more routine, your distractive behaviors are slowly stripped away and discarded. Even behaviors you consider harmless, or even necessary, will slowly become less important and will fade away as you mature and develop spiritually.

The second connection point on the spiritual journey, after recognizing and acting upon the initial invitation to enter into a relationship (the call), is to learn to develop the skill of paying attention to life. You can deepen your conviction to focusing your attention, awareness, and mindfulness, which will lead you to a more disciplined life. Awareness will develop when you choose the spiritual practice and the discipline that accompanies and supports it.

If you engage the second point of connection, you will slowly grow in daily awareness of the need to fully participate in life and not experience life as something that "just happens." The practice and the discipline that you will experience will lead you to the next connecting point of the journey.

The Wisdom of Jesus

I assert a position about Jesus' ministry that may startle some. His ministry was not about evangelization. It was charismatic and evangelical, but Jesus did not focus on relaying information to others about beliefs they may not hold. That kind of strict evangelization is certainly one of the ministries of the Christian community, the Church, but it was not necessarily the ministry of Jesus. He preached and taught more profoundly, with grace and purpose.

Jesus was not focused on catechetical formation or dogma. He wished to inspire a change of heart in the people, a change of purpose and a reordering of how they understood their world.[3]

When you read and reflect on the gospels and on the lives of the people of the early Christian communities, I think you will recognize that these people believed in God. They also desired, more than anything else, to lead lives in an intimate relationship with the God of their ancestors. The people Jesus lived with were people of the covenant. Like us, they tried, to the best of their ability, to lead lives of faithful service to God and one another.

They were also focused and disciplined people who were trying to learn the skills and practice the disciplines of their beliefs and rituals to the best of their ability. Not all were well led. Some were distracted from what was essential and necessary to deepen their intimate connection with the Holy One. Some of the paths proposed to them by religious leaders as helpful were actually lifeless, sometimes in the extreme.[4]

Jesus, a spiritually mature person, offered his followers a way of life that contradicted many of their familiar beliefs and rituals. For example, although he treasured and revered the observance of the law, he also recognized that observance of the law was not always life-giving. He accused the scribes and the Pharisees: "They tie up heavy burdens [hard to carry] and lay them on people's shoulders, but they will not lift a finger to move them. All their works are performed to be seen" (Matthew 23:4–5). At such times, he demonstrated frustration, while at other times, he revealed a deep sadness as he perceived the results of their feeble efforts. "His heart was moved with pity for them because they were troubled and abandoned, like sheep without a shepherd" (Matthew 9:36).

In his wisdom, Jesus did not engage in a full debate with those who espoused the entrenched positions, although they tried to trap him into such a discussion. Rather than debating the specifics, Jesus offered a new vision to the people who were willing to listen to him, using vivid illustrations to make his point. "The lamp of the body is the eye. If your eye is sound, your whole body will be filled with light; but if your eye is bad, your whole body will be in darkness. And if the light in you is darkness, how great will the darkness be" (Matthew 6:22–23). With illustrations and parables that inspired his apostles and disciples to perceive life in another way, Jesus called each person who followed him to wake up and see in a completely different manner. He called them to a deeper spiritual maturity on the path to a full life. Some responded with "yes," while others said "no."

The unwillingness of some of Jesus' contemporaries to attempt a new way of seeing and living certainly disappointed Jesus. There were also men in official leadership positions who went beyond reluctance. These religious leaders accused Jesus of demonic activity on more than one occasion. This constant refrain was more than likely devised in the halls of power in Jerusalem by men who wanted to keep their control and influence. With these men, Jesus went dramatically beyond lamenting and pronounced condemnation. "Therefore, I say to you, every sin and blasphemy will be forgiven people, but blasphemy against the Spirit will not be forgiven. And whoever speaks a word against the Son of Man will be forgiven; but whoever speaks against the Holy Spirit will not be forgiven, either in this age or in the age to come" (Matthew 12:31–32).

Contextual Commentary

It is not at all unusual, even in casual conversation, to hear people proclaim to family, friends, or acquaintances, "I am a spiritual person, but I am not very religious." Westerners generally view this as the summary statement of a person who no longer participates in organized religion. What people proclaim with this sentence is that they have not necessarily abandoned their relationship with God. It is also possible that they still consider many of the dogmas associated with denominational beliefs important and necessary. However, for a variety of reasons, they no longer feel the need or have the desire to be associated with a community of believers in a formal way.

Some people will continue to identify themselves socially as Catholic, Methodist, members of the United Church of Christ, etc., although it often mainly describes the traditional religious commitment of their families or upbringing. But this identification no longer plays a significant role in their lives or daily activities, writes Phyllis Tickle in *The Great Emergence: How Christianity Is Changing and Why.*

I propose that "spiritual but not religious" (SBNR) is peculiar to Western culture and society. No such distinction between religious tradition and culture and spiritual expression is ever seriously imagined in Buddhist, Hindu, or Confucian societies. In Muslim-dominated societies, I think such a distinction would be unacceptable and even dangerous. In decades past, the people of Western cultures may have privately considered themselves SBNR, but, at that time, it was culturally and socially impossible to proclaim without great personal risk.

As a person who is both spiritual and religious, I believe SBNR often goes right to the heart of what it might mean to be a committed and a spiritually mature person. This statement does not always describe a lived reality, as some people make such a proclamation almost casually, while it is a principled position for others.

SBNR may define a particular spiritual practice for some. For others, it may be a reaction to what some people believe to be serious contradictions and unsustainable doctrines within Christian denominations. In the minds of still others, it may go directly to the heart of what the *Catechism of the Catholic Church* acknowledges as "the scandal of bad example on the part of believers" (*CCC* 29), introduced in the first chapter.

SBNR might indicate admirable spiritual maturity. In support of this position, I offer for consideration the point of view of some psychologists and social scientists. I do not think it either wise or prudent to ignore the work of so many obviously gifted men and women and the results of their studies in reference to human beings and religious aptitude.

The work of Ken Wilber, for example, and his Integral Institute have proposed serious ways for modern people to be both religious and spiritual. One proposal, which he admits may be difficult for religious leaders to accept as important, is that "authentic spirituality must be based on direct religious experience." In other words, Wilber writes in *A Theory of Everything: An Integral Vision for Business, Politics, Science, and Spirituality*, if organized and denominational religion can learn to emphasize the heart and soul of the human and the divine, then religious expression invites people to participate in the deep meaning of the spiritual domain that is infused throughout daily life. Is this not what Jesus invites those who are willing to "enter through the narrow gate" to experience (Matthew 7:13)?

Although this idea may be sobering to some, and a negative summary in the minds of others, I find it wonderfully challenging. I believe that those who have arrived at a personal awareness of their own innate sense of the spiritual have already connected, at least in some manner, with the Holy One, the presence of Divine Mystery. Once connected, they are ready to continue their spiritual journey. All they need is some guidance and direction.

Disconnect

In the natural course of events, when people desire to focus their attention on spiritual matters and concerns, the most obvious way is to make a connection with a particular religious denomination. People reasonably assume that a focused and organized religion will provide the necessary community, support, rituals, dogmas, and practices that will enable their own spiritual practice and discipline. As a person who has enjoyed committed and lifelong religious participation, including a religious profession and ordination within the Roman Catholic tradition, I certainly support and encourage such a decision.

However, consider this: The best that any religious tradition or practice can offer you is only an incomplete picture and an imperfect response to the presence of Divine Mystery. When people attempt to speak about God, they cannot possibly do an all-encompassing job. There is so much more that is beyond human comprehension and humanity's ability to explain or dogmatize. Or, as the *Catechism* teaches, "Admittedly, in speaking about God like this, our language is using human modes of expression; nevertheless, it really does attain to God himself, though unable to express him in his infinite simplicity. Likewise, we must recall that 'between Creator and creature no similitude can be expressed without implying an even greater dissimilitude,' and that 'concerning God, we cannot grasp what he is, but only what he is not, and how other beings stand in relation to him'" (*CCC* 43).

When people walking the spiritual path forget that the presence of Divine Mystery cannot be completely explained or contained, there is an "unconscious"[5] temptation to abandon the spiritual journey. Once this happens, people may then try to satisfy their hunger by memorizing and following the rules and regulations of their denomination. Rigidity, a strict fundamental interpretation of denominational expressions, often results in the false belief that some things can be perfectly and even completely knowable.[6]

While this reaction is understandable, it is also unfortunate. The wonder, mystery, and awe of the presence of Divine Mystery cannot be duplicated or effectively explained or managed by any one system of beliefs, no matter how amazing. Adam B. Seligman, in *Modernity's Wager: Authority, the Self, and Transcendence*, writes, "A God that can be grasped, a God that can be conceptualized, is not a God." Further, I believe one of the greatest saints in the Catholic tradition and a Doctor of the Church, St. Thomas Aquinas (1225–1274), illustrates this point well.

After a brilliant career in which he produced literally millions of words explaining the mysteries of faith and religion, Thomas one day experienced the presence of

God in an entirely different manner. This experience led him to pronounce, "All that I have written seems to me like straw compared to what has now been revealed to me." From that moment on, he put down his pen and did not write any more. He died just three months after this experience, and so there is no way of knowing if he would have eventually written again.

I believe it is accurate to state that he did not disconnect from his relationship with God, and, from that singular moment forward, he understood this relationship in a completely different way. Moreover, he did not attempt to explain what he had experienced. For a man of his talent and academic achievement, who dedicated himself to trying to explain the unexplainable, this decision must not have come easily to him. It seems out of character. It also speaks of the power of the experience itself and suggests something of the awe and mystery that it must have inspired in him.

The temptation to effectively disconnect from the spiritual journey and satisfy religious needs with denominational orthodoxy and perfection is a temptation for many people. It is an even stronger temptation for people who are entrusted with the formation and teaching of other people: the clerical and professional ministers. The consequence of this kind of disconnect is one of the animating energies behind the observation recorded in Mark. The gospel reports that the people consistently contrasted the teaching of Jesus with the teaching of the scribes and the Pharisees: "What is this? A new teaching with authority" (Mark 1:27). The people who enjoyed the privilege of listening to Jesus seemed to sense the difference between his teaching and the teaching of their religious leaders, and many were drawn to the teaching that gave them life. It was not the teaching of the scribes and functionaries, but rather the teaching of Jesus, that appealed to them.

This kind of disconnect is not limited to people who are on a spiritual journey; it can also happen to those who believe they are not on a spiritual journey. People who have replaced the dogmas and doctrines of religion with equally strong rules and regulations in other forms of human thought and sciences can also fall prey to the same experience. I recall one of the conclusions expressed by the famous astronomer and lecturer Carl Sagan, a man who prided himself on his agnostic stance toward life, in his book *Pale Blue Dot: A Vision of the Human Future in Space*:

The earth is a very small stage in a vast cosmic arena. Think of the rivers of blood spilled by all those generals and emperors so that in glory and in triumph they could become the momentary masters of a fraction of a dot. Think of the endless cruelties visited by the inhabitants of one corner of the dot on scarcely distinguishable inhabitants of some other corner of the dot. How frequent their misunderstandings, how eager they are to kill one another, how fervent their hatreds. Our posturings, our imagined self-importance, the delusion that we have some privileged position in the universe, are challenged by this point of pale light. Our planet is a lonely speck in the great enveloping cosmic dark. In our obscurity—in all this vastness—there is no hint that help will come from elsewhere to save us from ourselves. It is up to us.

I sense sadness in this observation, and, at the same time, I also sense a possible disconnect with the principles and theorems of astronomy. Would not the vastness of the universe and what seems noticeable suggest there is so much more that is beyond our ability to understand? I find myself wondering, *Where is the invitation to discover what is beyond the "small stage in a vast cosmic arena"? Where is the imagination, the energy, and conviction that might fuel future discoveries of what is beyond a person's sight*? It seems to me that these are the kind of questions that need to be asked and that might be asked by someone either on the spiritual journey or drifting away from the spiritual journey.

Remaining connected to the spiritual path requires committed spiritual practice and discipline. Whatever form that practice takes is unimportant; it is the commitment to the practice that is essential. The necessary components of the practice include the two connecting points (responding to the call and learning to focus attention) that we have already discussed and the four connecting points that we will discuss in the following chapters.

Chapter Two Notes

1. The spiritual practice of attempting to be as fully aware as possible in the present moment, the "now," is extremely difficult. The moment you remember the now, that moment becomes the past. The moment you anticipate the now, that moment becomes the future. Being completely present to the now is to be present to the moment without memory and without anticipation; to simply be present, not measuring, judging, or anticipating the experience.

2. In *Evangelii Gaudium* (52), Pope Francis writes, "In our time, humanity is experiencing a turning point in history, as we can see from the advances being made in so many fields. We can only praise the steps being taken to improve people's welfare in areas such as health care, education, and communications. At the same time, we have to remember that the majority of our contemporaries are barely living day to day, with dire consequences. A number of diseases are spreading. The hearts of many people are gripped by fear and desperation, even in the so-called rich countries. The joy of living frequently fades; lack of respect for others and violence are on the rise; and inequality is increasingly evident. It is a struggle to live and, often, to live with precious little dignity.

3. In *Jesus: An Historical Approximation*, José Antonio Pagola writes, "The environment around Jesus in Israel is very different. All pious Jews begin and end the day by confessing their God and blessing his name. According to the historian Flavius Josephus, 'Twice a day, early in the morning and as the time for sleep approaches, they recall thankfully before God all the

things God has done for them from the time they left Egypt.' This custom of morning and evening prayer was already well established in Jesus' time, both in Palestine and in the Jewish diaspora. All men were obliged to practice it from age thirteen on. Jesus probably never went a day in his life without praying in the morning at sunrise and in the evening before he went to sleep."

4. Other proposed paths included those who followed John the Baptist and who longed for an apocalyptic solution, the end of time; the Zealots, who favored armed insurrection; and the Essene community, who withdrew in disgust from the culture and sought refuge in the desert, to name a few.

5. I say "unconscious" here because I believe that this inclination to satisfy human spiritual longing and connection with the presence of Divine Mystery through the perfection of denominational expression is not necessarily the result of a deliberative and reflective process of coming to a decision. I think if a person would deliberate, he or she would likely not abandon the spiritual journey but rather commit to it in a robust way! People who drop spirituality seem to "slide into it" in the first place because it seems right, and society accepts and even praises the decision.

6. As a Christian, I acknowledge and accept that in the Incarnation of Jesus Christ, the whole of God's truth has been made manifest. (See *CCC* 2465.) I also believe that the fullness of the Incarnation will never be fully explained until the end of time, and I try to live my life in participation of the continued life-giving manifestation of God's gift of grace.

Aware and Awake

The Movement from the Less to the More

"Spirituality means waking up. Most people, even though they don't know it, are asleep.... They never understand the loveliness and the beauty of this thing that we call human existence."

ANTHONY DE MELLO, SJ, *AWARENESS*

"If the inner self is awakened it communicates a new life to the intelligence where it lives, so that it becomes a living awareness of itself. And this awareness is not something that we have, but something that we are. It is a new and indefinable quality of our living being."

THOMAS MERTON, *WHAT IS CONTEMPLATION?*

"A man approached the Buddha, curious about his teachings and his life. The man asked the Buddha, 'Who are you? Are you a man?' 'No,' the Buddha replied. 'Are you God?' 'No, I am not God.' In frustration, the man then challenged the Buddha, 'Who are you then, neither man nor God?' 'I am awake,' the Buddha replied."

BUDDHIST STORY

"But you, brothers, are not in darkness, for that day to overtake you like a thief. For all of you are children of the light and children of the day. We are not of the night or of darkness."

1 THESSALONIANS 5:4–5

Awakening to More

The Christian Scriptures are filled with events, experiences, and teaching stories. Each of these memories of the believing community that preserved them is intended to inspire the reader to respond to the word of God. Each memory provides some understanding of the reasoning behind its inclusion in sacred Scripture. These memories also provide readers with insight and direction for their spiritual journey.

Widening the consideration and perspective beyond the Christian tradition, the sacred books of all spiritual traditions do the same, each in their own way. Spiritual masters, speaking from their own traditions, attempt to illustrate and share key concepts that they have learned in their own quests and that they hope will teach people about spirituality and the spiritual journey. While examples from a variety of spiritual traditions illustrate this point, the teaching of Jesus is perhaps the most useful and helpful.

In the Gospel of John, Jesus, challenged by the critical chorus of the scribes and Pharisees, answers them by stating, "Whoever follows me will not walk in darkness, but will have the light of life" (John 8:12). In another place, this time teaching his disciples, Jesus states,

"The lamp of the body is your eye. When your eye is sound, then your whole body is filled with light, but when it is bad, then your body is in darkness. Take care, then, that the light in you not become darkness" (Luke 11:34–35).

In each instance, and in many other examples that can be discovered easily in the New Testament, Jesus teaches his audience to see life in a new way, to focus their attention, and to appreciate the little things in life ("Notice the ravens" [Luke 12:24a]). He also instructs his disciples to learn to step back from the details of life and understand how they are related to the bigger picture. "They do not sow or reap; they have neither storehouse nor barn, yet God feeds them. How much more important are you than birds!" (Luke 12:24b).

With such straightforward teachings and encouragement, Jesus invited his audience to learn simple lessons. In his easy-to-comprehend stories, Jesus could teach all people about the necessity to focus. Some people were able to understand; others seemed incapable of understanding.

The Christian Scriptures, through the teachings of Jesus, the writings of St. Paul, and the pastoral letters, propose a challenging spiritual lesson. But unless readers develop a sensitivity to the context, they can get lost in the dogmatic translations and interpretations of the text. This lesson, first presented to the apostles and disciples of Jesus as an invitation, is to try and live life firmly rooted in an expectant faith. It is an invitation to see life as a gift that demands active participation and awareness, not something to endure.

When people encounter and practice the truth of this kind of living, a radical transformation takes place. Those who respond to the invitation become people "not of the darkness but of the light." The moment when this insight is awakened and claimed, people begin to focus their attention and live lives of mindfulness. They then experience the next connecting point on the spiritual journey, or, in the words of Jesus, they begin to experience the kingdom of God. It is also at this point that people can begin to understand one of the central teachings of Jesus: "For whoever wishes to save his life will lose it, but whoever loses his life for my sake and that of the gospel will save it" (Mark 8:35). Up until the moment when people make this connection, in cooperation with the abundant grace of God, this teaching may not make sense.

The stories and teaching of Jesus are not the only reference for this third connecting point on the spiritual journey, identified in some traditions as "awakening" and in others as simply "waking up." The process can easily be identified in all kinds of people and circumstances, once individuals understand what they are looking for. In each instance, the process of awakening begins with focused attention and awareness but then goes a step further, to recognition of how all of life is related and integrated. To put it another way, people learn to recognize "the more instead of the less." A few other examples from the wide variety of human experience might be helpful.

In Frank Herbert's *Dune*, a science-fiction classic, there is a scene in which the hero prince, a member of the Fremen community that is indigenous to the planet, confronts the leader of the priestly class with the accusation, "You are unwilling to drink of the water of life because it brings you to a place where you dare not look." Of course, the hero prince is willing to drink the water of life, and he is willing to investigate the place where the priestly class will not look, and because of his action, he experiences a profound change. "The sleeper has awakened."

What the hero prince experiences because of his

awakening is the ability to integrate all of life, not just a small part of it. The prince can see the big picture and make the connections, experiencing "the more instead of the less." Unfortunately, the priestly class, who we might assume to be spiritual masters, don't take the necessary steps on the spiritual journey. They are trapped with "the less instead of the more."

In the Acts of the Apostles in the New Testament, we find another story of awakening, one familiar to Christians. Saul, on the road to Damascus, encounters "a voice from the heavens" that he firmly identifies and believes to be the Risen Christ Jesus. Readers are not completely sure of all the details, and there is obviously more going on in this encounter than Acts records, but the result is that Saul, now renamed as Paul, experiences a profound change in his life. As the Scripture relates, "He regained his sight" (Acts 9:18). He moves from the darkness, where he cannot see, into the light, where he can see. From that moment on, Paul experiences the more instead of the less. He transforms from Saul, the fire-breathing persecutor of Christians, into Paul, the inspired evangelist and preacher of all things universal and cosmic that relate to the person of Jesus, the Risen Christ.[1]

As poignant and as powerful as Christian stories are, one of the most compelling spiritual tales of awakening is that of Prince Siddhartha Gautama, the Buddha. *In The Wings to Awakening*, Thānissaro Bhikkhu includes the prince's story.

Approximately 500 years before the birth of Jesus, the prince, or *bodhisattva* (Buddha-to-be), was living a life of tremendous wealth and refinement in northern India, where his every need or desire was immediately attended to by a servant. Despite his tremendous wealth, he had a stirring within, a desire for something more, and an understanding of what true happiness was: a happiness that was not dependent on his "intoxication with life" but on something much more profound.

To discover the truth of what he sensed within himself, it was necessary for him to escape from his life of pampering and luxury. It is interesting to note that he was not trying to escape luxury; he had nothing to compare it to. He was specifically intent on responding to the restlessness within himself. He sensed something was incomplete. It appeared he had everything anyone could want, but he believed there was much more to experience.

When he finally escaped his gilded cage and encountered life in a completely different way, everything changed, and nothing was ever the same for him again. The specific questions that led him to continue his quest—after what had to be the initial shock and disbelief of his encounter with life outside the walls of wealth—were the inevitability of aging, illness, and death. This led the Buddha to discover, through his focused attention and meditation, a new understanding. He discovered a truth that he then shared with others who also sought to be released from that which bound them to unhappiness. The Buddha lived the more instead of the less.

Each of these accounts exemplifies what it means to make this necessary spiritual connection. Becoming aware, and in the process entering deeper into the experience of spiritual maturity, is to arrive at a point where you experience a new way of seeing life. Obviously, this new way of seeing will be defined differently by a Christian, Buddhist, Muslim, or Jew. However, regardless of how it may be explained and understood, every person who makes this connection will be significantly changed in the process.

No matter how a person may understand or interpret his or her awakening, there seems to be a common element that is an essential component of the spiritual journey. When a person experiences what it means to be awakened, when a person moves from the less to the more, that person will immediately become more profoundly aware. This new awareness is well beyond that person's imagination. The following exercise might be helpful to illustrate this point for you.

Start the exercise by finding a comfortable place where you know you will not be disturbed or easily distracted. Next, make yourself comfortable while you think about a time in your life when you felt good. Sit with this life experience for a few moments, paying attention to the feelings it produces within you. Next, choose an instance that was not particularly positive or life-giving. As before, sit with this life experience for a few moments while you pay attention to the feelings that it produces. Contrast the good with the bad as you recall the feelings associated with both experiences.

After a few moments of reflection, refocus your attention on each experience. This time, consider each experience not from the narrow perspective of how you felt but within the broader picture of how it is part of the fabric of your life. Integrate the experience and make connections.

The purpose of the exercise is to help people become aware of how they can create their own environment by the things they choose to focus their attention on. When people learn both to focus on the details of life (awareness) and to step back from the details and consider the whole moment (awakening), they become less driven by anxiety and emotion and more open to the possibilities of life, health, and holiness.[2] Embracing awareness and awakening is how you experience the more instead of the less.

Another illustration of what happens in this process is illustrated by a popular animated movie, *Antz*. In the movie, we are introduced to a worker ant that is one among thousands. This ant is struggling to find his identity; he is trying to win the heart of the princess, whom he worships from afar, and eventually he is even called upon to save the colony from impending doom. Watching the movie, we are witnesses to the drama and struggle of life. Within moments, we are caught up in the frenzied activity of the colony, the quest for power and love, and the anxiety felt by the hero ant as he embarks on his adventure.

The spiritual lesson that *Antz* so beautifully illustrates comes at the end of the movie. As the camera slowly pans out from the activity of the colony, we learn that we have been watching the activity of a small anthill in the middle of a field. The camera pulls back a little more, and we see that the anthill is in the middle of Central Park in New York City. The camera keeps pulling back, revealing more of the city, the surrounding countryside, and eventually Earth itself, freely floating in space and surrounded by the rest of the universe. All is put into perspective as we see that the ants—and us—are all part of the "big picture." It is a powerful lesson. All of us count, big and little.

As you incorporate the spiritual practice of awakening in your life, you will recognize that you are slowly becoming someone who is trying to put all of life into the proper perspective, someone who is trying to live a life that is fully awake and engaged, someone who is trying to see the "more" of life instead of the "less." You want to "see the big picture"[3] without getting bogged down in the little things and the distractions of life. As you participate in this process and continue to commit your attention and energy to the rhythm of moving from the less to the more, you will notice the presence of certain experiences, at least two of which need explanation.

First, you may start becoming aware of an almost insatiable appetite for knowledge and a variety of different perspectives. Second, as you make more connections and become more comfortable with integrating the events, choices, and judgments of life into a wider perspective, you may feel a kind of "intoxication," which is both serious and measurable. Intoxication is the direct result of consuming too much of a particular substance. Here, the "substance" is knowledge or perceived knowledge and/or experience over a short period of time. The body and spirit simply do not have enough time to properly digest what you've consumed, so they become overwhelmed.

The experience of an insatiable appetite and the intoxication that often results are distractions on the spiritual path. It is a lesson that has been referenced in the spiritual journey of the Buddha, but it is certainly not limited only to his experience. These distractions are potential dangers for each person on the journey.

If you are in the beginning stages of becoming awake, you may want to read and study more about the spiritual experience, such as the many forms and manifestations of spirituality that may be discovered in different spiritual traditions. You might become interested in attending spiritual retreats. You might visit the spirituality section of the bookstore, looking for a book on a topic that has just captured your imagination. In a real sense, you may become a consumer of spiritual thought, practices, and experiences, never arriving at the point where you experience fullness or satisfaction.

As the intoxication continues, another component may arise: a form of arrogance can become a real part of your experience. This arrogance includes the impatience and frustration you may feel toward others in your life who are not making the connections they should be making or who seem unable to see their issues clearly. Sometimes this frustration leads to real conflict, and, in some extreme cases, it even leads to circumstances that might end long-standing relationships or friendships.

Unfortunately, the cultural wars that are raging have turned the value and purpose of this kind of movement into a negative instead of a positive. "Wokeness" is the current buzzword for things viewed with suspicion and disgust by people who find themselves with a different perspective. Although there always have been and always will be different points of view, what makes this reaction difficult to comprehend is the anger that seems to fuel it. From my perspective, this anger is puzzling at the core.

Movement and emerging truth should be core values of the human spirit. The more we learn about ourselves and our relationship with the universe, the more integrated we will be. To lose the desire to widen our horizons and stretch our spirits and imaginations would mean throwing away the most sacred of all gifts and graces. To resist seeing, to resist moving from the less to the more, is the same kind of reaction demonstrated by the scribes and Pharisees in the time of Jesus. It was ultimately self-defeating then, and it will be today.

A word of caution directly related to spiritual intoxication is necessary at this point. An intoxicated person is highly vulnerable and prone to manipulation. What is true about intoxication with alcohol and drugs applies to spiritual intoxication, perhaps even more so. The effects of spiritual intoxication are no less profound than those of intoxication by substances, and the after-effects are no less startling. If there is any significant difference, it is that spiritual intoxication lasts longer than a weekend or a one-night bender on booze or drugs.

Because intoxication makes people more vulnerable

to suggestion, a drunk person might jump off a bridge if told that he or she could fly. The intoxicated person is also much more open to manipulation and thus may be exploited by unscrupulous people or those intent on fermenting chaos or any other kind of disruption. This kind of manipulation of the spiritually vulnerable may even be presented within the framework of high-sounding religious imperatives, with glorious and eternal rewards promised in return.[4] How often, when confronting the aftermath of an act of terrorism, will people ask, "What would make a person do this?" It is perhaps more accurate to ask, "Who would manipulate a vulnerable person to do this?"

While we know the spiritually intoxicated are vulnerable and more easily manipulated, and thus more prone to dramatic actions, there are also many examples of behaviors that are significantly less dramatic but nevertheless important to acknowledge. For example, people new to a denominational community initially are often the most enthusiastic volunteers and participants, sometimes committing themselves to projects and responsibilities that are well beyond their capacity to fulfill.

People in their mid-twenties or early thirties often

consider full-time ministry as one possible response to their new relationship with a religious denomination. Sometimes, they know they have been called; at other times, only the experience of novitiate and/or seminary clarifies the situation for them. In each instance, it is helpful to remember that these people are good people, with the best of intentions, who desire to answer the call of God. However, despite their inner goodness, they are vulnerable because of intoxication. It is not sustainable, and eventually, when the "buzz" wears off, they find themselves confused and disorientated.

When reality dawns, the feelings of intoxication are often replaced with feelings of regret and self-doubt, which can be even more powerful than and potentially as harmful as the intoxication. Decisions made from this perspective also carry a high risk of being unhealthy and non-life-giving. People in this situation need middle ground, the experience of the ordinary and the stable, with as much drama eliminated from the equation as possible.

Spiritual Direction

A spiritual mentor, guide, or director—a spiritually mature person familiar with the spiritual journey—is extremely helpful at this time. That is not to suggest there is no role for a spiritual director in less dramatic times, but the path forward is particularly perilous if the person is unaccompanied on his or her journey. Many potential pitfalls, false directions, and even significant emotional intensity can be part of the journey, so the strength and guidance of another person is appropriate.

Saint Teresa of Ávila (1515–1582) is perhaps the strongest example of this point. Even though she was a great saint and mystic, renowned to this day for her spiritual insights and practices, it was not until she received the direction and support of another great saint and mystic, St. John of the Cross (1542–1591), that she was able to secure the kind of spiritual direction she needed. Recalling her somewhat difficult process of encountering many would-be directors who seemed not to understand what she was experiencing, the saint exclaimed, "I'm sick and tired of those people who go about saying, 'The devil, the devil, the devil,' when instead they should be saying, 'God, God, God.' I fear these kinds of people more than the devil himself." Still later, she explained that, given a choice, it would be better to have a learned director who is not very holy than to have a holy director who is not learned.

The history of saints, not to mention the history of ordinary men and women, is littered with countless examples of people who have experienced unhelpful spiritual direction. A single distinguishing characteristic, as St. Teresa underlines, is a lack of knowledge. An even greater risk is a would-be spiritual director or mentor who is more interested in waging "theological battles" or championing "ideological positioning." When a mentor's knowledge of the spiritual journey is clouded with prejudice and opinions, he or she is effectively blind to the workings of the Spirit.

Choosing a spiritual director is important. It is not simple. Take the same care as you would in choosing a doctor. Your director, mentor, or companion must be one with whom you can establish a relationship of honesty and full disclosure. He or she must be a person with whom you can talk openly and who respects your spiritual values. The person must be familiar with and have knowledge about the religious tradition you follow.[5]

You may want your director to have convictions that are representative of your denomination. Within the Roman Catholic tradition, many prefer direction from a priest, deacon, or vowed religious man or woman.

This choice often reflects the seeker's need to be reassured of the denomination's "orthodoxy." On the other hand, some may seek a director with a contrasting spiritual background, giving a "point/counterpoint" flavor to spiritual direction.

Hopefully, with the expertise of spiritual direction from a mentor who can help you navigate this part of the spiritual journey along with the potential risks of arrogance and intoxication, your movement from the less to the more will be a life-giving and invigorating connection to a spiritual practice and perhaps a religious discipline. Ultimately, however, although you may not imagine or understand when you first experience it, this point of connection is only another step on the path. This connection is most certainly not the place of completion or where the journey should end. Regardless of how you might feel at this point, what is to come is even more powerful and even more life-giving.

The Wisdom of Jesus

When I reflect on the experience of awakening—the movement from the less to the more—I often recall the example and wisdom of Jesus. Several times, Jesus ministers to his disciples by sending them to preach, to heal, and to announce the coming of the kingdom of God. They return exhausted and with a sense of fulfillment, but the stories also suggest something more.

> *So they went off and preached repentance. They drove out many demons, and they anointed with oil many who were sick and cured them…. The apostles gathered together with Jesus and reported all they had done and taught.*
>
> *He said to them, 'Come away by yourselves to a deserted place and rest a while.' People were coming and going in great numbers, and they had no opportunity even to eat. So they went off in the boat by themselves to a deserted place.*
>
> *People saw them leaving and many came to know about it. They hastened there on foot from all the towns and arrived at the place before them.*
>
> MARK 6:12–13, 30–33

Reading a little between the lines, the apostles returned to the Lord, eager to share with him their adventures and their experiences. In another place, they respond, "Lord, Lord, did we not prophesy in your

name? Did we not drive out demons in your name?...
Did we not do mighty deeds in your name?" (Matthew
7:22). Heady stuff, certainly enough to focus their attention and to provoke their excited response. And what is
Jesus' response to their excitement and perhaps intoxication? As we see in the foregoing Scripture passage, he
invites them to withdraw and reflect on what they had
experienced.

At that time, Jesus recognized that his apostles did
not need additional ministry or more experiences of the
powerful outpouring of the grace of God. What they
needed most was the experience of rest and reflection
to put into perspective what had occurred. To respond
in any other manner would have been counterproductive; it would not have helped the apostles connect with
and appreciate where they were now positioned on their
spiritual journey.

This was not the only example in which Jesus sought
a place of solitude and rest for himself and his disciples;
in fact, it happened often and became an essential component of the experience of discipleship. It is important
for us to recognize the need for silence and solitude in
all of life, but particularly in the spiritual life.

Silence and solitude are essential for reflection, developing perception, and ultimately coming to a personal understanding of the meaning of life. Socrates once remarked, "The unexamined life is not worth living." We might not agree with the fullness of his conclusion, but certainly the truth of his statement is appropriate.

Contextual Commentary

The spiritual masters delight in retelling a story I find useful. An old monk, standing outside the monastery one day, is asked by a younger monk, "Why is it that so many people seemingly begin the spiritual journey but do not persevere in their quest?" At that moment, a rabbit, pursued by a pack of dogs, runs by in front of the master and the questioning monk. There is a slight pause, and then another pack of dogs comes running past them. The old monk smiles, looks to the younger monk, and says, "Observe what happens next." Sure enough, after a few moments, one of the dog packs returns to the village, yapping and barking all the while. The master tells the young monk, "That yapping and barking pack of dogs is the same pack of dogs that went by us a few minutes ago. They never saw the rabbit; they just heard the barking. And so it is with the spiritual journey. Some people start the journey, but they never actually see the rabbit. As a result, they soon grow tired and discouraged. To stay committed to the journey, you have to see the rabbit and not just follow the barking."

As you continue along the many steps of your spiritual journey, you should slowly sense within yourself that you are moving away from being spiritually intoxicated. You should sense that the arrogance, and the perceptions and judgments that may result, become less and less operative each day. This progress can also be identified and understood as the movement from the less to the more. It is a powerful experience.

If, on the other hand, you experience no movement or progress and instead remain in the stage of intoxication, you must become focused again. As the story about the rabbit and the dogs informs us, either you have taken your eyes off the rabbit, or you never saw the rabbit and have been just following the barking.

If you, the spiritual seeker, have been working with a spiritual director, that director will, hopefully, guide you to experience even more richness in your spiritual quest and journey. The next step is not something that your director will force you to experience. It is something your director should recognize within you and help you respond to with the appropriate focus and attention. You and your spiritual director will sense that it is time to move forward when you feel certain indications in your inner core, such as a tugging, an invitation, and a restlessness.

Disconnect

As you might imagine, spiritual intoxication is the greatest single risk to the continued commitment and discipline required for walking the spiritual path. This intoxication, which emerges from accumulating many spiritual thoughts, practices, and experiences, can become the focus of your spiritual journey and thus effectively disconnect you from a deeper spiritual maturity and practice. The accumulation often has the same effect in other areas of life. The study of addictive substances and behaviors and the effects of addiction on people is revelatory and provides us with a helpful reference point.

One of the signs of addiction is that the behavior or substance, such as alcohol, that initially produces the sought-after buzz is not enough to sustain the desired effect. Let's say a person needs to drink one ounce of alcohol to feel its effects. As the addiction progresses, soon he or she needs to drink two ounces to feel the effects, then three ounces, and so on. It is the same with any addictive behavior. An addictive gambler may start out being satisfied with a $1 bet and a $100 win. Eventually, however, the $1 bet gives way to a bigger bet, with greater risk, so that the winnings can be more substantial. The "high" experienced with the bigger win is contrasted with the devastation of the bigger loss, and the person is tossed from one extreme to the other.

Any experienced spiritual director will tell his directee that someone trapped in the snare of spiritual intoxication will repeat the same addictive behavior and process. This can consist of attempting to accumulate more spiritual practices, experiences, and even particular graces that some of the old spiritual traditions identify as "consolations."

Eventually, however, the person cannot maintain a spiritual high, and he or she seeks out spiritual direction as a remedy, often with an incorrect self-diagnosis of the condition. The person assumes that his or her perceived inability to feel the rush of emotion or satisfaction previously associated with spiritual practices is the "dark night of the soul,"[6] which is a very unfortunate, unhelpful, and inaccurate diagnosis. What the person is experiencing usually is not a dark night of the soul but perhaps a feeling of disillusionment like the one Peggy Lee sang about so hauntingly in "Is That All There Is?"[7]

Recovering from spiritual intoxication while being gently encouraged by a competent spiritual director will help you realize that you are experiencing an invitation to something more, not less. This realization can be discouraging if it is not placed within the most helpful context possible. You may be tempted to disconnect from the spiritual journey at this point, seeking solace and encouragement by reengaging with your former spiritual director. Here again, as is often the case, a good spiritual director can use this experience to invite you to continue moving forward.

As wonderful and powerful as spiritual consolations, feelings, and emotions can be, you can experience more richness on the journey. To depend on such consolations as a measurement of spiritual maturity or spiritual progress is an error in judgment.

The woman who illustrates this reality most powerfully is St. Teresa of Calcutta (1910–1997). After her death, her spiritual journals were edited and published, revealing that she endured a prolonged period where she felt no consolation, no attachment, and no feelings of comfort in her prayer. According to her journals, this situation continued for most of her life. As published in a 2007 *Time* article titled "Mother Teresa's Crisis of Faith," she wrote to a spiritual confidant, "Jesus has a very special love for you. As for me, the silence and the emptiness are so great that I look and do not see, listen and do not hear." With the possible exception of the atheistic author Christopher Hitchens[8], most people would agree that this lack of feeling, as severe as it may have been, did not seem to inhibit either her work or her commitment to faith. Few would suggest that Mother Teresa did not reach some level of spiritual maturity in her life.

It is important that her testimony be understood within the proper context. Early commentators often referred to her experience as the dark night of the soul, but it most assuredly was not. Any such reference was made by those who do not understand the dark night of the soul or the spiritual journey, and it was not good for them to assign meaning to her experience without comprehending it.

Mother Teresa's ministry was an inspiring lifelong demonstration of a contemplative union with God. Her work spoke volumes while she quietly accomplished it. Mother Teresa and God never separated, which is a crucial point. We know she never strayed from the Trinity because her purposeful efforts were continual. There was no discord. No doubt. No anxiety. Just a resolute confidence that enabled heroic commitment. That is why she is a saint. The extraordinary gifts of Mother Teresa to God and his people show us what an unbreakable connection to Divine Mystery can do. This will become ever clearer in the pages that follow.

Chapter Three Notes

1. Having your eyes opened and having the ability to see does not always feel good or beneficial. In Genesis, Adam and Eve have their eyes opened. It seems that the author of Genesis understood this ability to see as a characteristic of divinity and not necessarily a characteristic of humanity (Genesis 3:4–7). Later, Jesus seems to reject this perspective and invites people to see. More than once, Jesus restores sight to people (Luke 18:41–44).

2. This is an unpublished exercise from Kenneth Sedlak, CSsR, and the Pathways learning community. Used with permission.

3. The "big picture" is a constricted image used here to suggest that what is necessary is a person's ability to look beyond what is directly in front of him or her and instead try to assume a

perspective that considers more than just the obvious. The view shown by a telescope, focused tightly on a single planet, is enhanced when the focus is widened to include the stars around the planet and then the universe that supports the stars. The image shown by a microscope, tightly focused on a single cell, is enhanced when the focus is widened to include other molecules surrounding and supporting the cell. A telescope may offer a better view of the "big picture" because it reveals the universe, but a microscope has the same power in revealing the complex picture of life that is hidden from our sight.

4. Mark Juergensmeyer, in *Terror in the Mind of God: The Global Rise of Religious Violence*, examines the cases of a number of people who engage in or support the use of violence for religious ends in different religious traditions: Christian (reconstruction theology, Christian Identity, abortion clinic attacks, the Oklahoma City bombing, Northern Ireland), Judaism (Baruch Goldstein, the assassination of Yitzhak Rabin), Islam (World Trade Center bombing in 1993, Hamas suicide bombers), Sikhism (assassinations of Indira Gandhi and Beant Singh), and Buddhism (Aum Shinrikyo). He also interviews those who participate in or advocate religious violence, including Mike Bray, Mahmud Abouhalima, and others.

5. From Willigis Jäger, *Contemplation: A Christian Path* (quoting St. John of the Cross, *The Living Flame of Love*): "It is very important that a person, desiring to advance in recollection and perfection, take care into whose hands he entrusts himself, for the disciple will become like the master, and as is the father so will be the son."

6. The "dark night of the soul" is typically used to describe a phase in a person's spiritual life that is marked by a sense of loneliness and desolation. For our purposes, the possible experience of the "dark night" would be more appropriately referenced not at this point, but later on the spiritual path. Dark nights are more common and perhaps not unexpected when a person is connecting with silence, solitude, and conversion.

7. The lyrics of this existentialist song ("Is That All There Is?") are from the point of view of a person who is disillusioned with unique events in life. The singer tells the story of when she saw her family's house on fire when she was a little girl, when she saw the circus, and when she fell in love for the first time, expressing her disappointment in each experience.

8. Christopher Hitchens, author of *The Missionary Position*, a scathing polemic on Mother Teresa, and, more recently, of the atheist manifesto *God Is Not Great*: "She was no more exempt from the realization that religion is a human fabrication than any other person, and that her attempted cure with more and more professions of faith could only have deepened the pit that she had dug for herself."

CHAPTER FOUR

Nourishment

Entering Silence and Solitude

"Whenever there is some silence around you— listen to it. That means just notice it. Pay attention to it. Listening to silence awakens the dimension of stillness within yourself, because it is only through stillness that you can be aware of silence."

ECKHART TOLLE, *STILLNESS SPEAKS*

"When the Lord wishes to draw a soul to himself, he leads it into solitude, far from the embarrassment of the world and intercourse with men, and there speaks to it with words of fire. The words of God are said to be of fire because they melt a soul....In fact, they prepare the soul to submit readily to the direction of God".

ST. ALPHONSUS LIGUORI

"Barriers are sundered, fetters are melted
By the divine fire,
And the eternal dawn of a new life rises,
In all, and all in One."

VLADIMIR SOLOVYOV

"We need to find God, and he cannot be found in
noise and restlessness. God is the friend of silence. See
how nature—trees, flowers, grass—grows in silence;
see the stars, the moon, and the sun, how they move
in silence….We need silence to be able to touch souls."

ST. TERESA OF CALCUTTA

"Solitude and prayer are the greatest means to
acquire virtues. Purifying the mind, they make it
possible to see the unseen. Solitude, prayer, love, and
abstinence are the four wheels of the vehicle that
carries our spirit heavenward."

ST. SERAPHIM OF SAROV

"Entrench yourself in these traits I mention to you.
Solace, submissiveness, and silence, for they all bring
forth humility, which absolves all sins."

ST. ABBA ISAIAH

The Power of Silence and Solitude

Chapter Three ended with an illustrative example of Mother Teresa's contemplative unity with God and in her life and ministry. By examining the essential role and meaning of silence and solitude in the spiritual life and in the spiritual experiences that are dependent on the integration and integrity of these components, we might discover the truth and learn from it.

I became aware of the power of silence and solitude through a series of seemingly unrelated events. Because of these experiences, I eventually learned the important lesson that silence, and often the solitude that supports it, must be discovered, experienced, and then embraced. There is no shortcut, no other path.

Aware of the Silence

The first incident took place when I was about thirteen. I remember the day of discovery as a beautiful snowy morning in my home state of Michigan. I awoke earlier than the rest of the family, determined to get dressed in my winter clothing and venture outside. I immediately headed toward the wooded area behind our house to a special place that I had previously identified as a place of safety and comfort. It was a clearing within the woods, which always provided me with a sense of being alone, even though in reality I was surrounded by the city and the houses in our subdivision. When I arrived at my special place, I was struck by the crispness, the whiteness, and, most of all, by the silence.

I wasn't a particularly religious boy. That came much later. However, I was raised in a believing and traditional Catholic family. Our family was faithful to attendance at Mass and the other devotions, and that life experience probably contributed to my interpretation and perception that morning. Like other boys my age, I usually would have been distracted more easily by other thoughts, feelings, and emotions, yet the silence is what captured my attention and imagination that day.

I remember standing in the clearing and becoming centered and focused on the silence. I wondered how there could be so much beauty, so much whiteness, and so much wonderful silence. I also found myself relating this experience to my personal understanding of who God might be. I felt a dramatic tugging, almost an invitation, to somehow be in a more personal encounter with this God. The experience lasted for quite a long time, but eventually the combination of the cold and the fact that I had not eaten breakfast forced me to break the connection and return home. It was not until years later that I recalled and contemplated this introduction to silence.

My second meeting with silence, unrelated to the first, occurred almost ten years later. I was in the seminary chapel, attending a celebration of the Eucharist. Attendance at the Eucharist was a daily event, something not at all out of the ordinary. On this day, immediately after the reception of holy Communion, I discovered the same intimate stillness that I had first felt in the snow-covered clearing in the woods.

Although all sorts of activity surrounded me, such as the coming and going of the other seminarians to their assigned places, I remained focused on the silence within me and did not become distracted. When the Eucharist concluded, and the seminarians and faculty members began walking out of the chapel, I stayed. The intimate silence continued and deepened.

Because my religious training was a little more intense at this point in my life, I began to enrich the quiet with Scripture, praying the words of the Apostle Peter: "Lord, it is good that we are here" (Matthew 17:4). It was good to be in the silence, very good. I felt sincere in my prayer and totally at peace. I had no desire to change the moment. I was not the least bit anxious or fearful. I sensed that there was something special about the moment and that it was somehow important.

After the passage of a significant amount of time, I emerged from my privileged experience of silence and became aware of the sounds and other activity around me. Much to my surprise, I did not struggle or resist, even though I immediately recognized a sense of loss and disappointment. After a few more moments of simply lingering to see if anything else might occur, I left the chapel and returned to my normal routine. I shared what happened with my spiritual director, who did not recognize the moment for what it meant to me, dismissing it as unimportant. I let his comment keep me from referring to my time with silence in the chapel for a few years. But I treasured those moments and the ones in the snow—both unexpected happenings—in my heart.

My third experience of intimate solitude also took place without forewarning. While vacationing, I visited the site of some ancient Native American ruins just south of the city of Phoenix. I was with a group of friends, and we were touring the area, checking out the sites. I was not expecting a religious encounter.

I became separated from the group and was standing a little off the prescribed pathway. I was looking around, enjoying the beauty and solitude of the place, when I became aware that the power of the moment was not in the scenery. Although the desert landscape was beautiful, I recognized that silence had found me again. I was again in a relationship with intimate and sacred silence, again supported by solitude, with the silence and the solitude each dependent on the other but also secure in their own meaning. The voices and sounds of this tourist spot had been replaced with something completely different.

As I remained in what I felt was a convergence of reality and mystery, I became aware that the ground I was standing on was a sacred place. I have no way of knowing for sure, but I somehow sensed, in the silence, that this had once been a place where others had also experienced the presence of Divine Mystery. Though I had little in common with the people who had lived here, I sensed a connection with them. This connection seemed important to me, so I thought about what they might have experienced here.

Did the people who had been here centuries before me, who also had encountered the silence and solitude of the place, expect to have that experience, or was it unexpected? Did the ancient people come to this place of mystery and the sacred to be nourished, or did they have other reasons?

This encounter with sacred silence and solitude was brief, but it was dramatic, sacred, and simple. After a few minutes, I heard the voices of the other tourists, who were discovering the wonders of the ancient ruins, thus ending my silence. I knew that, once again, something important had taken place.

All three experiences of serenity were necessary for my spiritual growth. At that point in my life and on my journey, I was at least awake enough to recognize the importance of these moments. And, for the first time in my life, I was self-reflective and mature enough to place all three silent moments into a context that helped me grow spiritually.

At the same time as my encounter in the desert, I was also blessed with a spiritual director who was well-versed in the nuances of the spiritual journey. I was happy to find someone who understood what had happened to me. His own spirituality helped me dig into my experience for all it could teach me. In learning, I was invited to an even greater understanding and thankfulness.

My three moments of silence nourished my spirit when I least expected it. I have learned that in encounters with silence and solitude, the invitation to be part of the experience is profoundly present and life-giving. Also, I now understand that the experiences, as they unfolded, could not be controlled or predicted; I was invited only to accept them as a manifestation of grace.

I am amazed at how often people in all walks of life have similar things happen to them. I am even more amazed at how many times people have encountered such silence but have misunderstood, mistrusted, or ignored it. Similarly, it's unfortunate when a person is blessed with this kind of encounter and then shares it with a spiritual director who is unfamiliar with the manifestation of the Divine Mystery. The spiritual and the sacred surround us. We should learn to see it, trust it, and freely permit it to nourish and animate us.

As wonderful as it is to feel the intimacy and sacredness of silence when we least expect it, we can also experience the power of silence when we seek it deliberately. Spiritual maturity begins to grow within us when we realize that we meet God most profoundly in the quiet, not in the accumulation of ideas or knowledge. In those uncluttered moments, I felt God's presence deeply.

Greater spiritual maturity can take place when a person begins to emerge from his or her spiritual intoxication. When the spiritual traveler lets go of the need to consume as many new ideas and encounters as possible, real growth and connection can happen. When a person celebrates the encounter with the sacred, the presence of Divine Mystery—the presence of God within him or her—is recognized. When it dawns on the seeker that everything he or she has been collecting and experiencing is, in fact, nothing more than distractions, it becomes easy to discard the unnecessary and seek what provides the fullness of life.

We find an example in a favorite story from the Hebrew Scriptures, which tells of the prophet Elijah's encounter with God in what we might call a mystical experience:

> *Then the LORD said: Go out and stand on the mountain before the LORD; the LORD will pass by. There was a strong and violent wind rending the mountains and crushing rocks before the LORD—but the LORD was not in the wind; after the wind, an earthquake—but the LORD was not in the earthquake; after the earthquake, fire—*

but the LORD was not in the fire; after the fire,
a light silent sound. When he heard this, Elijah
hid his face in his cloak and went out and stood
at the entrance of the cave.

1 KINGS 19:11–13A

Elijah, perhaps because he was a prophet and well versed in the ways of God, or perhaps because he just sensed it, understood that his encounter with God would take place in the quiet, the place where he could distinguish the "light silent sound." The heavy winds and the crushing rocks were dramatic, as was the earthquake, no doubt, but the meeting with God happened in the stillness, after the drama.

Silence provides the necessary space for communication, discovery, and continued growth that we need in our relationship with the presence of the Divine Mystery. Silence invites each person to learn, to make the necessary connections in life. Silence and solitude are necessary conditions for becoming aware of the ultimate truths of life and relationships. Silence is "food for the soul"—the essential nutrient that fuels our spirits. Just as people cannot survive without food and water for long, so the soul cannot survive and thrive without the essential presence of silence and the solitude that supports it.

Alive in Solitude

Silence leads to a way of living that can best be described as contemplative.[1] Without contemplation, our response to the sacred would be incomplete and unfulfilling. Deprived of the contemplative experience, a person would ultimately be led further away from intimacy rather than becoming fully engaged in the relationship with Divine Mystery. In search of the environment that supports us and encourages us to fully experience silence—the essential nutrient of the spirit/soul—a person will discover the need to seek out solitude.

When I stood in the clearing in the woods so many years ago, I did not realize that I was being nourished. When I was invited into the ultimate silence and connection with the presence of Divine Mystery in the seminary chapel or when visiting the ruins outside of Phoenix, I did not yet understand the intensity of the grace in which I was being invited to participate. I did not yet understand that to fully drink in the nourishment I was offered, I needed to seek out a place of solitude, where I could be alone with the presence of Divine Mystery.

Walter Savage Landor (1775–1864), an English poet, commented on the power of solitude in his *Imaginary Conversations*: "Solitude is the audience chamber of God." Amelia E. Barr (1831–1919), a British-American writer, observed in *All the Days of My Life*, "We hear voices in solitude, we never hear in the hurry and turmoil of life; we receive counsels and comforts, we get under no other condition." These authors understood and appreciated the need to withdraw, to seek out the conditions that are conducive to silence, and then to trust the experience.

Perhaps the most dramatic witness to the power of both solitude and silence at work is found in the lives of people who devote themselves entirely to cultivating the experience. *Into Great Silence*, a 2006 film from German filmmaker Philip Gröning, powerfully observed the day-to-day life of the Carthusian monks at Grande Chartreuse, which is considered one of the world's most ascetic monasteries. The film has no dialogue, no background music, nothing but the clear and powerful silence of the moment, and viewers are invited to contemplate the lives of these men as they move through their day. There are moments when they are at prayer with other monks and when they are silently at work in a monastery workshop or garden. But most profound are the hours they spend alone in their individual monastic cells, seeking only to contemplate and listen to the voice of the presence of Divine Mystery.

I watched this film with some of the members of my religious community. The intensity of the sustained silence and solitude vividly illustrates the challenge and the grace of each moment. Coming from days filled with the work of our own ministries, we were unable to watch the film in its entirety in one showing. We chose to watch the film over two evenings, and it was a wise choice. Even just watching, let alone living, the solitude portrayed in the film was a real struggle. It was difficult to sustain the necessary attention and awareness that would allow us to fully appreciate the lives and spiritual journeys of the monks.

By watching this powerful film, I discovered I had perhaps only dabbled in what I know and understand as essential for my own spiritual journey. Nevertheless, I was encouraged, not discouraged, by this realization. I understand and accept that I have only begun to drink from the well of nourishment that has been offered to me and to all who walk the spiritual path, seeking the presence of Divine Mystery.

For most people, the solitude offered by a monastic cell is unattainable, let alone desirable. For people who experience the push and pull of many daily responsibilities—such as raising children and providing for a family—it is perhaps even unimaginable. It seems to beg the question, *If solitude is so essential for spiritual growth and development, why is it difficult, if not impossible, to experience?* Is this some kind of cosmic joke? No, it's not—but it is true that finding solitude presents a significant challenge.

In our society, most people do not have the opportunities for prolonged periods of silence and solitude that our ancestors enjoyed not so many years ago. In fact, when modern humans occasionally experience prolonged silence or solitude in their lives, it is often due to something being broken. For example, storms can result in power outages, leaving us without electricity to power our appliances and gadgets. An eerie, almost dream-like sensation occurs when the power is out and nothing works. Nonetheless, such an experience shows us how we can begin to find what we need. In short, we should deliberately choose to "power down and power off" the noisemakers in our lives.

"Turning off" the noise in life is not as difficult as it

may sound. For example, how easy is it to get into a car, put the key in the ignition, and choose not to turn on the radio? Can we develop a habit of taking just a single moment before engaging the ignition to take a breath and consciously recall the presence of Divine Mystery in our lives? How about introducing fifteen minutes of silence after dinner into our family's routine? No television, no dishwasher, no computer. Each family member just selects a space to be quiet and alone for those few moments, maybe catching their breath, reading a book, or simply closing their eyes and relaxing. Before you swing your feet out of bed and onto the floor each morning, would it be difficult to take one minute to deliberately recall the presence of God in your life and thank him for the gift of life?

People who are not so busy, or those who have reached a time in their lives when prolonged silence and solitude are more easily attainable, should not waste the opportunity to make this essential spiritual connection. For people who have been called and gifted to live the religious life, or those engaged in some kind of ministry, the opportunity and the responsibility to respond to the call of the presence of Divine Mystery with a consistent practice of silence and solitude could not be any clearer.

Spiritual maturity depends on the essential nourishment that comes from a regular practice of silence and solitude. It is a significant sign of the beginning stages of spiritual maturity when we do not fear silence or become anxious when experiencing silence. The maturity that we seek means that we learn to participate in the moment and trust the experience.

The Risk of Clutter

Spiritual masters teach the necessity of "listening to the silence." In other words, they caution us not to pack our own personal agendas into the silence. It is so easy to clutter the silence and use this time to engage in all kinds of distractions, such as sorting out the meaning of life, trying to determine the best use of your talents and efforts, reciting prayers of intercession and directives to God, or praying the ritual prayers required by ordination or the wider call of ministry (for example, in the Roman Catholic tradition, praying the Divine Office). There are appropriate times for these practices and devotions, and they should most certainly not be abandoned. However, the time you devote to listening to the silence is not the appropriate time.

In addition to listening to the silence, the spiritual masters often speak about the clutter that a person can accumulate in the places of solitude. They caution us not to fill our chosen places for solitude with books, unfinished projects, computers, or other items that can provide us with comfort and purpose. In an area designated for silence and solitude, these things have no place.

Entering into silence and solitude means you are transitioning into a new dimension, a new connecting point. It is not necessary to bring anything you think you need into this experience, as these things are delusions, distractions, unnecessary baggage. Silence and solitude will provide you with all that is necessary.

Humility and Simplicity

In stark contrast with spiritual intoxication and the accumulation of spiritual consolation, silence and solitude do not easily distract. The disciplined practice of silence and solitude focuses you even more intensely on the spiritual journey.

Thomas Merton, in *New Seeds of Contemplation*, provides us with a glimpse into the intensity of the experience: "As a magnifying glass concentrates the rays of the sun into a little burning knot of heat that can set fire to a dry leaf or a piece of paper, so the mysteries of Christ in the gospel concentrate the rays of God's light and fire to a point that sets fire to the spirit of man. And this is why Christ was born and lived in the world and died and returned from death and ascended to his Father in heaven…through the glass of his humanity, he concentrates the rays of his Holy Spirit upon us so that we feel the burn, all mystical experience is infused into one soul through the Man Christ."

Although Merton is writing about the power of the Incarnation of Christ, the image of the magnifying glass concentrating the sun's rays into a "burning knot of heat" is useful for our consideration here. Sustained silence and solitude begin to "burn away" from us the roots of arrogance and our attachment to the accumulation of "things." In their place is the start of standing humbly before God, stripped of any thought or pretense, overwhelmed with the certainty that everything is a gift, everything is grace. Saint John of the Cross observed:

> *The weight of arrogance is such that no bird can*
> *fly carrying it. And the man who feels superior*

to others, that man cannot dance, the real dance when the soul takes God into its arms and you both fall onto your knees in gratitude, a blessed gratitude for life.

In the place of arrogance, conviction, and the comfort of your own gifts and talents, there is the profound feeling and experience of fragility and vulnerability. As frightening and as anxiety-producing as this may sound, the opposite is true. In fragility and vulnerability, there are no paralyzing fears or anxieties, even though you may feel that an essential part of your sense of self is being peeled away. You will sense, fortified and nourished by the sustained experience of silence and solitude, that there is no need to fear. Although you may not understand the full meaning of what you are experiencing, you will learn to trust the experience. You will know and understand that you are in the loving embrace of the presence of Divine Mystery.

As the feeling of the presence of Divine Mystery lingers, you will discover a sense of humility, a call to the simplicity of life, and the stirring of compassion. The desire to be compassionate is initially a reflection of your humanity.[2] It is an acceptance of responsibility for the perceptions and judgments that have become the lenses through which you view life, your sense of self, and your relationships with others. Eventually, however, this begins to develop into compassion for other people, including those you love and those you may not. The greater the silence, the deeper and more penetrating the grace.

As powerful and as necessary this experience is to the spiritual journey, it is best understood as an invitation to a greater and more dynamic movement through the power of grace. There is still so much more—a richness and an invitation to continue journeying.

The Wisdom of Jesus

Most Scripture scholars agree that the ministry of Jesus began with his baptism in the Jordan by John the Baptist. The scholars also agree that there is no historical certitude provided by the Scripture texts that provide the reasoning behind his decision to seek baptism from John. There is agreement that the event must have occurred because of the "criterion of difficulty."[3] The inclusion of this event in the gospels presented difficulty for the early Christians, who had some explaining to do in trying to answer the persistent questions: "Why did Jesus submit himself to baptism by John? Had Jesus sinned? Was Jesus somehow subservient to the Baptist?"

Because it is probably impossible to discern the reason for Jesus' sudden appearance at the River Jordan, it is perhaps more important to reflect on what we do know instead of what we do not know. For example, we know from Scripture that Jesus presented himself for baptism at the approximate age of thirty. He was from Galilee and an obvious craftsman or day laborer, marked by the rays of the burning sun and with hands that reflected a life of difficult labor. He was unmarried and unaccompanied. He was seeking an experience of the presence of God and was therefore attracted to the Baptist's preaching and the ritual of cleansing baptism that supported it.

The gospel stories also reveal the sequence of events that take place after Jesus appears at the Jordan. After John baptizes Jesus, Jesus has an awakening, a connection with the presence of Divine Mystery. This connection, perhaps also witnessed by the Baptist, produced a response in Jesus that may have frightened him or at least drove him to take a specific action. He turned from the river and the Baptist and fled into the desert, the traditional place where the people of Israel encounter God. The physical space of the desert and the religious significance of this space are of vital importance.

Although Jesus was unaccompanied during his desert sojourn, and there were no witnesses to the experience itself, the gospels offer the reader a summary of what occurred:

> Then Jesus was led by the Spirit into the desert to be tempted by the devil. He fasted for forty days and forty nights, and afterwards he was hungry. The tempter approached and said to him, "If you are the Son of God, command that these stones become loaves of bread." He said in reply, "It is written: 'One does not live by bread alone, but by every word that comes forth from the mouth of God.'"

> Then the devil took him to the holy city and made him stand on the parapet of the temple, and said to him, "If you are the Son of God, throw yourself down. For it is written: 'He will command his angels concerning you' and 'with their hands they will support you, lest you dash your foot against a stone.'" Jesus answered him, "Again it is written, 'You shall not put the Lord, your God, to the test.'" Then the devil took him

up to a very high mountain, and showed him all the kingdoms of the world in their magnificence, and he said to him, "All these I shall give to you, if you will prostrate yourself and worship me." At this, Jesus said to him, "Get away, Satan! It is written: 'The Lord, your God, shall you worship and him alone shall you serve.'" Then the devil left him and, behold, angels came and ministered to him (Matthew 4:1–11).

These temptations introduce us to the inner struggle of Jesus. It is a struggle made even more intense because it is magnified by the silence and solitude of the desert. His temptations to feed his hunger, to manipulate God, and to give in to the obvious distraction of losing his focus on the will of God are numbered. Each temptation is focused on something that cannot satisfy, despite promises to the contrary. It is perhaps helpful to understand these temptations within the context of the entire lived experience of Jesus as it was witnessed by his apostles and disciples. Each temptation illustrates the memory of the early Christian community as they remembered the struggles of Jesus. Played out in more than one event, these struggles were perhaps indicative and understood as a constant and persistent temptation to doubt.

The temptations of Jesus are memories of not only the temptation in the desert but also perhaps temptation at other times in his life. These struggles provide the reader with some understanding of what Jesus experienced in the silence and solitude of his own spiritual journey. The temptations illustrate some of what takes place as the inner soul and spirit are finely tuned for what is to come next. This story also underlines the need for remaining patient and steadfast in faith and in confidence, resisting the urge to do otherwise.

Contextual Commentary

Because I understand that silence is the essential nutrient of the spirit/soul, I am particularly concerned with the lack of sustained silence in many people's lives. Because so many people seem to be deprived of this essential nutrient, I sense that humanity may be on the cusp of what will soon be an epidemic of spiritual starvation. The presence of Divine Mystery will call and invite people to connect to the experience of the sacred, but people will not be able to easily hear the voice of and the invitation to mystery.

I am also growing in the conviction that the slaughter of so many innocent men, women, in children through gun violence, for example, is illustrative of the starvation already experienced. The uselessness of war and the carnage we see on our television screens are bluntly and dramatically illustrative of humanity that is lost— not just in need of redemption from sin, as the preachers will proclaim again and again in churches that are increasingly empty every weekend. It is much more profound, much more critical than we might imagine. We have an answer for sin and a tried-and-true method for repentance. What or who will restore humanity as a species to health and vibrancy? Or has humanity doomed itself?

Humanity's technological wizardry has presented us, collectively and individually, with so many wonderful gadgets and devices that have the potential to enrich our lives. Radios, televisions, computers, cell phones, electronic readers, and AI-powered virtual assistants are readily available for our use. The revolution of wireless connectivity makes these devices open to everyone, in even the most desolate of places with no infrastructure in place. Satellites far above us enable connection where it once was not possible or even conceivable.

These inventions and innovations help us navigate the world in which we live, connect each of us with our loved ones, enable us to serve our families and communities in emergencies, and fill up our free time with seemingly endless entertainment options. However, we pay a price when we engage with our devices; unfortunately, that price is far beyond the dollars and cents we pay for them.

If you live your entire life with some sort of device plugged into your ear, pounding out the latest news, information, or soundtrack, is it just—as Neil Diamond might say—"beautiful noise"? We are now experiencing whole generations of people who are "wired for sound." People seem to be unaware of any potential consequences. Yet, if silence is truly the essential nutrient of the soul, will the price we pay be much more than we could ever imagine?

There are consistent reports that a person's hearing can be damaged, sometimes permanently, by the overuse of technological devices. But that damage may be only the beginning of the story. We are ignoring a much larger concern. How will humanity be molded or changed when we are wired to the unrelenting onslaught of noise? How will spiritual, integrated, and holistic people be formed when we are continually deprived of the sound and the silence of the natural world? How will humanity survive as a self-reflecting species when people are spiritually malnourished to the point of starvation? Perhaps the alien cybernetic race known as the Borg, the omnipresent enemy and scourge of humanity in the Star Trek series, is not that far-fetched after all.[4]

Disconnect

Deep within the Christian tradition of spirituality, and as seen in the story of the temptation of Jesus, we can encounter the stories of people who dedicated their lives to the pursuit of silence and solitude. In these stories, we are invited to reflect on the many spiritual struggles that emerged from the silence and solitude. Core components of these wisdom stories are the demons that were seemingly their constant companions. These demonic forces are portrayed as powerful, wrestling with the desert sojourners to discourage them in their spiritual practice and commitment. Often, a demonic force assumed a form suggestive of a particular temptation or vice; for example, enticing the spiritual seeker to break his or her fast from food or engage in some sort of forbidden sexual behavior.

In today's world, most people are reluctant to assign responsibility for their spiritual struggles and difficulties to the work of demonic forces. However, despite this reluctance, the reality is that people undergo significant external and internal struggles because of their desire to connect with the spiritual path. While people may not identify these challenges and struggles as demonic, they can be very present and real.

We can consider the following tough questions in relation to encounters with silence and solitude:

- *If connecting to the spiritual path is so important, and if spiritual maturity is so desirable, why is it so difficult?*

- *If the presence of Divine Mystery truly desires to be in relationship with humanity as a whole and singularly with individuals, where is the encouragement to persevere?*

- *Why do so many people begin the spiritual quest but then abandon the effort?*

Based on observable behavior, I think people may desire spiritual maturity, but only a small number of people attain it. The disciplined contemplative practice required for even the beginning levels of spiritual maturity only makes sense to a person who believes that, fundamentally, people are created to be selfless, not selfish. The desire to connect to the spiritual path is the desire to become whole. To possess, even briefly, the spark of life within, a person must withstand a certain amount of emotional, physical, and spiritual pain and suffering. The testament of so many saints and others who have journeyed before us demonstrates that this is inescapable.

There are also, by extension, the emotional, physical, and spiritual pleasures of life that sustain people on their journeys. Perhaps, as the spiritual masters teach us, the key to spiritual maturity is not to dwell on what separates a person but rather what unites a person—to consciously and deliberately seek unity with other humans, with nature, with the world, and with the spirit/soul that animates every man, woman, and child.

Are these satisfactory answers? For some, they undoubtedly provide a limited sense of satisfaction. For others, these answers are significantly lacking as a convincing position. Still others may be convinced that the confrontational so-called demonic tormentor is persisting in the attempt to draw people away from the spiritual journey so they will settle for something incomplete and unfulfilling. It has always been this way.

Jesus told his disciples and apostles that "your heavenly Father…makes his sun rise on the bad and the good and causes rain to fall on the just and the unjust" (Matthew 5:45). They did not want to hear this. They wanted Jesus to tell them about their reward for being righteous and the retribution and the justice they could anticipate when the Reign of God came upon them. They wanted Jesus to repeat to them what their religious leaders preached, but Jesus adamantly declined to do so. Jesus invited his disciples to come to his way of thinking. He knew that the meaning and importance of life has nothing to do with rewards, or the lack thereof. Life is more profound. The rejoinder "what's in it for me?" misses the point of life.

We can easily hear the voices of demons in an endless variety of events and experiences. Only in listening to the silence can we hear the voice that calls and invites each of us to something more.

Chapter Four Notes

1. Thomas Merton, in *New Seeds of Contemplation*, writes, "Contemplation is life itself, fully awake, fully aware that it is alive. It is a spiritual wonder. It is a spontaneous awe at the sacredness of life, of being.... It is gratitude for life, for awareness, for being. Contemplation is above all, awareness of the reality of the source of life."

2. See Ephesians 4:32: "Be kind to one another, compassionate, forgiving one another as God has forgiven you in Christ."

3. The criterion of difficulty, the criterion of discontinuity, the criterion of multiple witnesses, and the criterion of consistency are often applied to the study of Scripture to help determine the importance and the authenticity of a particular text. Any basic introduction to the study of Scripture text helps us understand and appreciate how these criteria are universally applied.

4. The Borg, a fictional pseudo-race of cybernetic organisms, is depicted in the *Star Trek* series. They operate solely to fulfill one purpose: to "add the biological and technological distinctiveness of other species to [their] own" in pursuit of perfection.

CHAPTER FIVE

Conversion

A Change in Attitude and Perception

"Go ahead, light your candles and burn your incense and ring your bells and call out to God, but watch out, because God will come, and he will put you on his anvil and fire up his forge and beat you and beat you until he turns brass into pure gold."

—SANT KESHAVADAS, QUOTED BY JACK KORNFIELD
IN *AFTER THE ECSTASY, THE LAUNDRY*

"'Neither fear nor self-interest can convert the soul. They may change the appearance, perhaps even the conduct, but never the object of supreme desire... Fear is the motive which constrains the slave; greed binds the selfish man, by which he is tempted when he is drawn away by his own lust and enticed' (James 1:14). But neither fear nor self-interest is undefiled, nor can they convert the soul. Only charity can convert the soul, freeing it from unworthy motives."

—St. Bernard of Clairvaux

"Conversion is not the smooth, easy-going process some men seem to think.... It is wounding work, of course, this breaking of the hearts, but without wounding there is no saving.... Where there is grafting there is a cutting, the scion must be let in with a wound; to stick it on to the outside or to tie it on with a string would be of no use. Heart must be set to heart and back to back, or there will be no sap from root to branch, and this I say, must be done by a wound."

—John Bunyan,
THE EXCELLENCY OF A BROKEN HEART

"Every authentic religious epiphany or encounter, every true experience of God, in whatever form, makes a person less insular, less complacent, and less isolated—and more restless, more inspired, and more engaged with the world and humanity."

—FR. ANTHONY J. GITTINS, *A PRESENCE THAT DISTURBS: A CALL TO RADICAL DISCIPLESHIP*

"Every authentic experience of truth and goodness seeks by its very nature to grow within us, and any person who has experienced a profound liberation becomes more sensitive to the needs of others."

—POPE FRANCIS, *EVANGELII GAUDIUM* (THE JOY OF THE GOSPEL), 9

What Is True Conversion?

In the religious sense, conversion[1] is the call to change, to repent, or to begin a new way of living. It is a dominant theme in both the Old Testament and the New Testament. The prophets of the Old Testament often challenged the people of Israel to change their ways. They invited the people to abandon one type of living and live in a different way—a way that was more in line with the prophets' definitions of what was essential and necessary for the people of the covenant. The call to repent, and to see and hear things the way that the Lord sees and hears, can be illustrated by the prophet Isaiah: "You deaf ones, listen, you blind ones, look and see! You see many things but do not observe; ears open, but do not hear" (Isaiah 42:18, 20).

In the New Testament, John the Baptist picks up the prophetic theme of change and repentance—"Prepare the way of the Lord, make straight his paths" (Matthew 3:3)—but adds a twist: John requires a ritual baptism with water for those who have received his message and, as a result, have acknowledged sinfulness in their lives. Jesus expands the message of John early in his ministry, proclaiming, "Repent, for the kingdom of heaven is at hand" (Matthew 4:17). Jesus, in contrast with John, requires no ritual action but rather offers a reason and a vision, both of which he explains when speaking about the kingdom of God. Jesus' reason and vision have always inspired some and repelled others.

In the Christian tradition that developed from the ministry of Jesus, "conversion" has become a loaded word for some when used in a spiritual context. Conversion has been influenced by consistent preaching over the last 2,000 years that emphasizes sinfulness and the ever-present need for people to convert and change their lives. But there is something in the imagined experience of conversion that may not initially attract a person and may even be seen as something to avoid or ignore.

When some people hear the word "conversion" and think about the concept of conversion, they immediately associate it with taking specific action in their lives, which they may perceive negatively. Some automatically assume that they will be challenged to change, and the call to change often produces feelings of guilt, incompleteness, inadequacy, or discouragement.

Given the long history and practice of conversion, these perceptions and feelings are understandable but also unfortunate. Conversion as a root spiritual value has little to do with changing a person's specific actions or activities. It has everything to do with changing a person's attitude and outlook. To emphasize actions or activities distracts the person from the real purpose value of conversion. It is really a matter of understanding and appreciating where the emphasis should lie, because misplaced emphasis can lead a person to frustration instead of to integration and the fullness of life, which are the true intentions of conversion.

A powerful story from the life of Jesus illustrates this point. Many know it as the story of the "good thief." It takes place when Jesus is close to death.

> *One of the criminals hanging there reviled Jesus, saying, "Are you not the Messiah? Save yourself and us." The other, however, rebuking him, said in reply, "Have you no fear of God, for you are subject to the same condemnation? And indeed, we have been condemned justly, for the sentence we received corresponds to our crimes, but this man has done nothing criminal." Then he said, "Jesus, remember me when you come into your kingdom." He replied to him, "Amen, I say to you, today you will be with me in Paradise."*

> LUKE 23:39–43

Interpreters sometime emphasize the comments of the "good thief" in contrast to those of the "bad thief." The good thief, who knows that he did wrong and that Jesus is innocent, accepts his fate. He knows that God will soon have something to say about all of this, because his own death and final judgment are imminent. The bad thief, on the other hand, shows little acknowledgement or acceptance of what is happening and persists in his "bad" behavior.

In the traditional interpretation of the story, Jesus saves the good thief because he repents. We are encouraged to assume that the bad thief is not saved because he does not repent. We often feel some sort of satisfaction when we interpret the story in this way. It fits into our concept of what conversion might be about. The good thief converts, even if it is at the last moment.[2]

But what happens if the story is not about anything the thieves did or did not do? What happens to our understanding of the story if this scene is not about conversion in the way we might define it? What happens to our interpretation and perception when we realize the story is not about conversion but about the generosity of God? Indeed, conversion is more about generosity than it is about repentance or justice.

When we open our vision to a new way of seeing, we realize that this story and others about Jesus tell us he was a wise, generous, loving, and forgiving man. Period. From the Christian perspective, Jesus is all of this because he is God and represents the Abba God. Jesus invites people to be in relationship with the Abba God of the promised kingdom of God. His invitation is not one of worn-out ideas of right and wrong. Punishment and reward are not the primary experiences within the kingdom.

If the story is really about the generosity of God—and I believe it is—can we learn anything about conversion from it? Yes. But remember, the emphasis is not on the actions of either the good thief or the bad thief. To learn the lesson, we must see the generosity of God.

The "good thief story" illustrates the point that conversion is not so much an action but an attitude. This attitude toward life permeates a person's vision and understanding, enabling the most generous and surprising reaction possible from the converted person. Perhaps this attitude can affect any reality, even in moments of great trauma and personal suffering.

With this new way of looking at conversion, Jesus continues to inspire his disciples with his vision of the kingdom of God and models the converted attitude that the story teaches. With this generous point of view, a converted person could turn his or her attention to the bad thief, who has lost it all, rather to the good thief, who is promised heaven. Once your attention is focused on this unfortunate man, the question becomes, "What generous, loving, and forgiving thing is God going to do for him?"

Even though conversion is not about action and activity, a converted person will try to live a life in which their personal actions and activities represent a meaningful change of perception and focus. Remember: conversion is an attitude. It is a way of seeing and living life that animates a person's daily decisions. If you embrace this attitude as a defining and essential stance in your life, you will experience not only the need to repent and have a change of heart but also the need to see as God sees and to be as generous as God is.

Seen this way, conversion is the connection, the growing awareness that is fueled by silence and solitude. It is the point of convergence. Conversion is the result of becoming aware and awake, of looking at the "big picture." It is a person's resistance to being narrowly focused, convinced of his or her own limited opinions and judgments. Conversion takes place in the silence and the solitude, the place where a person encounters God, the presence of Divine Mystery. Conversion is where each person understands and accepts that it is "not our way, but God's way." The following parable from the life of Jesus further illustrates the point.

The Gospel of Matthew tells a story about the owner of a vineyard who goes out at different times of day to hire workers to work in the vineyard. He goes out early in the morning, at mid-morning, at noon, at mid-afternoon, and right before the end of the workday. Every time, the owner finds workers who need employment, so he sends them to go and work in his vineyard.

The kingdom of heaven is like a landowner who went out at dawn to hire laborers for his vineyard. After agreeing with them for the usual daily wage, he sent them into his vineyard. Going out about nine o'clock, he saw others standing idle in the marketplace, and he said to them, "You too go into my vineyard, and I will give you what is just." So they went off. [And] he went out again around noon, and around three o'clock, and did likewise. Going out about five o'clock, he found others standing around, and said to them, "Why do you stand here idle all day?" They answered, "Because no one has hired us." He said to them, "You too go into my vineyard." When it was evening the owner of the vineyard said to his foreman, "Summon the laborers and give them their pay, beginning with the last and ending with the first." When those who had started about five o'clock came, each received the usual daily wage. So when the first came, they thought that they would receive more, but each of them also got the usual wage. And on receiving it they grumbled against the landowner, saying, "These last ones worked only one hour, and you have made them equal to us, who bore the day's burden and the heat." He said to one of them in reply, "My friend, I am not cheating you. Did you not agree with me for the usual daily wage? Take what is yours and go. What if I wish to give this last one the same as you? [Or] am I not free to do as I wish with my own money? Are you envious because I am generous?" Thus, the last will be first, and the first will be last.

MATTHEW 20:1–16

In this story, the owner pays the workers in an atypical way. Usually, the first people hired are paid first and sent on their way, and those who were hired later wait for their turn. This reversal of the way payment is traditionally made is deliberate. Jesus fully understands that people will immediately pay attention to what occurs next in the story, because they know that the story intends to make a point. They sense that the lesson will be important and dramatic.

As the foreman begins paying the workers and calls forth those who came last to the vineyard to receive their wages first, there may have been some grumbling among the other workers. Quickly the grumbling gives way to anticipation when the workers observe that those who had worked only a short time got a full day's pay. As you read the story, you can almost sense their initial confusion, then their building excitement. *If someone who worked only a short time gets paid a full day's wage, I wonder what those of us who bore the brunt of the heat and the sun all day will be paid?* As more workers are called forth, and as each is paid the same wage, the anticipation turns to boiling rage and a sense of being swindled. This is exactly the kind of reaction Jesus was hoping for as he unraveled the parable for his listeners:

he wanted them to feel the same way that the workers in his parable were feeling.

"Do I not have the right to be generous?" the owner retorts when confronted by the anger of his remaining workers. (Undoubtedly, the others had left as quickly as possible, knowing full well what was going to happen.) The answer from the seething workers seems to be, "No, you do not have a right to be generous. Not at my expense!"

It is not at all unusual for people, upon hearing this story, to assume that it is about the generosity of God, primarily because generosity seems, in a casual reading of the text, to be the vineyard owner's focus. However, the reversal of how the workers get paid indicates there is something more going on in the story. If the parable's purpose was to illustrate the owner's generosity, the owner could have paid those who came first the agreed-upon daily wage and then paid those who came last the same amount. Those who had borne the heat of the day would have been long gone and would never have witnessed how much the others were paid. When the workers who came last were paid a full day's wage, it would have made the point that the owner was generous. The dramatic reversal indicates that the story has a different audience. It is intended for those who have been present from the beginning and who have labored all day: the disciples of Jesus.

People could certainly persist in believing that the story is primarily about the vineyard owner's generosity and, by extension, the generosity of God. However, could people also see the parable as an example of the real cost of conversion—the change of attitude and perception that Jesus requires of his followers?

Is it too much of a stretch to believe that Jesus told this story to teach his apostles and disciples about the necessary attitude and perception of a person who lives in the kingdom of God? Seen in this way, the story challenges Jesus' followers to identify with, but not to imitate, the people who worked in the vineyard all day. Jesus wants the workers to rejoice that the others benefited from God's generosity, not to complain about God's generosity and feel shortchanged. He wants them to rejoice that they witnessed such beneficence, even if it means that they had to work hard all day for the same amount of money as those who worked fewer hours.[3]

Another parable from Matthew further illustrates the meaning of conversion. Here, as in many other teaching parables of Jesus, notice how he reverses the assumed roles and reactions of the people in the story to produce the intended lesson for his listeners.

The kingdom of heaven may be likened to a king who decided to settle accounts with his servants. When he began the accounting, a debtor was brought before him who owed him a huge amount. Since he had no way of paying it back, his master ordered him to be sold, along with his wife, his children, and all his property, in payment of the debt. At that, the servant fell down, did him homage, and said, "Be patient with me, and I will pay you back in full." Moved with compassion, the master of that servant let him go and forgave him the loan. When that servant had left, he found one of his fellow servants who owed him a much smaller amount. He seized him and started to choke him, demanding, "Pay back what you owe." Falling to his knees, his fellow servant begged him, "Be patient with me, and I will pay you back." But he refused. Instead, he had him put in prison until he paid back the debt. Now when his fellow servants saw what had happened, they were deeply disturbed, and went to their master and reported the whole affair. His master summoned him and said to him, "You wicked servant! I forgave you your entire debt because you begged me to. Should you not have had pity on your fellow servant, as I had pity on you?" Then in anger his master handed him over to the torturers until he should pay back the whole debt. So will my heavenly Father do to you, unless each of you forgives his brother from his heart.

MATTHEW 18:23–35

For members of the parable's original audience, the idea of a king—a man of the privileged class—being generous to a servant would have required a significant stretch of their imagination. This was certainly not the expected behavioral pattern of a man in charge, as discussed in José Antonio Pagola's *Jesus: An Historical Approximation*. For a servant to receive generosity and understanding instead of misery and punishment was also unheard of. The audience would have been flabbergasted to think such a scenario was possible.

Yet, just as they permit themselves to imagine what it might be like to experience such a blessing, Jesus introduces another encounter, a familiar one that was played out every day. The servant who has been forgiven the massive debt is also the holder of the debt of another person, albeit significantly less than what he himself had owed the king. What would happen next?

Jesus is leading his audience to the point where they are required to compare the massive debt owed by the servant to the king to the minuscule debt owed to the servant by one of his peers. He desires his audience to imagine for a moment how relieved and blessed the newly enriched and forgiven servant might be to the person who was in debt to him. Surely, the servant who had received such a blessing and such a bounty just moments earlier would extend the same to his fellow servant. However, that was not the case. The servant has no mercy, no understanding, and no forgiveness of the tiny debt. Rather, he unleashes whatever power he has on the other servant. The audience is outraged, and rightly so. "This judgment cannot stand. This wrong must be made right."

What happens next is crucial, as Jesus presents us with the final reversal of the parable. The outraged servants report to the king what has happened, and the king withdraws his generosity. He orders full punishment and misery on the servant who he had once blessed. It is in this action that the teaching of the parable is revealed, and the listeners understand that the story is about conversion: changing a person's attitude and perception. This parable invites those who hear the story to learn a new way of living and a new way of seeing: You have all been blessed abundantly by your heavenly Father in ways you can never repay because the debt is too enormous. Therefore, be generous and loving to one another as your heavenly Father is generous and loving to you.

This story also speaks eloquently about how difficult it is to change a person's thoughts, opinions, and judgments. The servant who received a great blessing from the king is so disconnected from the reality of what it means to be grateful, generous, and compassionate to another that he is unable to instinctively give even a small portion of what he had been given to someone else. No one would disagree that it was not right for him to demand payment of the debt that he was owed. But to demand payment of a tiny debt after getting a great and unexpected gift? How could he be so callous, so unaware, so dulled in his experience of life and love that he could think it acceptable to act like this?

These and other parables incorporate the principle of reversal by which Jesus teaches his followers about the change in attitude and perception that is required of them. Jesus preached that this change is what truly animates a person who seeks to live in the kingdom of God. The new attitude and perception of conversion helps a person comprehend some of Jesus' other teachings. When asked by Peter, "'Lord, if my brother sins against me, how often must I forgive him? As many as seven times?' Jesus answered, 'I say to you, not seven times but seventy-seven times'" (Matthew 18:21–22). Or, "For whoever wishes to save his life will lose it, but whoever loses his life for my sake will find it. What profit would there be for one to gain the whole world and forfeit his life? Or what can one give in exchange for his life?" (Matthew 16:25–26). In each instance, Jesus challenges his followers to convert an existing attitude into a new way of seeing and believing. Many people in Jesus' time enthusiastically believed this message. Some found it difficult. It is the same today, 2,000 years later.

The Christian Scriptures provide examples of the true meaning of conversion and the generosity of God. Some of these examples show a person's reaction when they do not receive a message well.

Jesus' story of the rich young man is one of the most illuminating stories about conversion in the New Testament. It is a tale of a person who was invited to conversion but did not accept the invitation, and it is as powerful now as it was when Jesus revealed it.

An official asked [Jesus] this question, "Good teacher, what must I do to inherit eternal life?" Jesus answered him, "Why do you call me good? No one is good but God alone. You know the commandments, 'You shall not commit adultery; you shall not kill; you shall not steal; you shall not bear false witness; honor your father and your mother.'" And he replied, "All of these I have observed from my youth." When Jesus heard this, he said to him, "There is still one thing left for you: sell all that you have and distribute it to the poor, and you will have a treasure in heaven. Then come, follow me." But when he heard this, he became quite sad, for he was very rich. Jesus looked at him [now sad] and said, "How hard it is for those who have wealth to enter the kingdom of God! For it is easier for

*a camel to pass through the eye of a needle than
for a rich person to enter the kingdom of God."*

LUKE 18:18–25

The rich man lives a moral and upright life. He upholds the commandments and tries his best to follow the will of God. Someone hearing this story for the first time might think the man had no reason to convert because he seemed to be living and acting in the right way. However, the call to conversion was not a call for the man to change his actions, but rather to change his attitude, his perception of life, his heart. Jesus recognizes the man's basic goodness and challenges him to conversion, to change his way of seeing. But this man was unable to make the change. He could not convert. He could not accept Jesus' invitation.

The rich young man in the story is not a bad person. He is spiritual and tries to live an upright and blessed life. At the same time, we can conclude that despite his goodness, despite his efforts, something was missing.

In the silence and solitude of prayer, through the guidance of the Spirit of God, people are invited to the experience of conversion. Some people's perceptions, attitudes, and judgments will easily be converted. In many instances, a person will shed some of his or her quirks and habits quickly, like a reptile shedding its old skin. However, others will be unable to shake their old habits and get rid of material possessions, believing that these things help define them. Their conversion may take longer, if it happens at all.

Anthony de Mello, SJ, a Jesuit author and spiritual director, relates a story about his personal development and spiritual journey in his book *The Song of the Bird*. He says that at one point in his life, people told him he needed to change because he was perceived as anxious, depressed, and self-centered. As a result, he tried to change and was urged on by his best friend and many acquaintances. However, no matter how hard he tried to make the changes that were important to him and to others, he was unable to do so. One day, Anthony's friend said to him, "Don't change. I love you as you are." After hearing those words, he reports, "I relaxed. I came alive. And suddenly I changed! Now I know that I could not have really changed until I found someone who would love me whether I changed or not."

De Mello's experience mirrors that of many men and women. It emphasizes a basic starting point for making any change. What is the lesson here? It seems that, before a person can make any real progress in spiritual maturity and growth, the person must be reassured and confident that he or she is loved. Being loved does not guarantee maturity and spiritual growth. The person still needs to work hard. But the reassurance that "I am loved" enables the process.

To love and to be loved requires a willingness to trust, to accept vulnerability, and then to enter intimacy. Becoming spiritually vulnerable and intimate means coming to a point where you are willing to stand before the presence of Divine Mystery with nothing hidden, with no perceptions or judgments, and with no requirements. It means becoming immersed in the fullness of real life and love. This kind of trust, vulnerability, and intimacy is often a terrifying experience for people. The inner self cries out in panic, believing that accepting the divine will result in oblivion—absorption into nothingness. Although the fear is real, the feared result is not. The real outcome of vulnerability and intimacy is to feel the dying gasp of the false self as the true self struggles to be born. It is true that "in order to gain your life, you must be willing to lay down your life."

The fear of losing everything can both paralyze and energize. When it is a paralyzing fear, it can render a person argumentative, depressed, isolated, lethargic, and more. It can also produce negative physical reactions, such as sleeplessness and loss of appetite. When this fear energizes people, it can produce the opposite effect, leading them to make significant and dramatic life changes through the grace of God.

Martin Luther (1483–1546), a key Christian reformer, shows us what fear can do to a person. His spiritual story begins with overwhelming fear and ends with a spirited conviction in faith. His story, including his struggles, has nourished millions.

As a young, reasonably devout man, Luther devoted himself to the pursuit of a solitary commitment: to encounter the presence of Divine Mystery. As an Augustinian monk, inspired by the mystical tradition of his day, which encouraged the silent contemplation of God or the experience of peace of heart, he was without peer. However, despite his commitment to the discipline of silence and contemplation, he encountered terror, not peace. He feared for his own death. He writes, "I, who horribly feared the last day," found no peace and no encouragement. He was overwhelmed with the fear of everlasting punishment and found no intimacy, no encouragement, that would lead him to a different conclusion. His health deteriorated, and he had one sleepless night after another. This paralyzing fear carried him to the threshold of despair, as Richard Marius discusses in *Martin Luther: The Christian Between God and Death.*

Luther was eventually freed from his fear and developed an energizing faith by embracing his belief in the abundance of God's grace. This newly claimed belief enabled him to arrive at a point in his own faith journey and spiritual growth where he became absolutely convinced of God's love for him, as quoted in Marius' book: "For I know One who suffered and made satisfaction in my behalf. His name is Jesus Christ, the Son of God. Where he is, there I shall be also." His understanding of grace was that the power of the Holy Spirit of God was consistently capable of bringing a person to the fullness of life and love and to salvation.

Luther's spiritual story goes far beyond theology. He was a man of his time and place, and the turbulence of history surrounded him. His actions and choices, and those decisions implemented in his name or in support of his positions, were certainly not universally welcomed. Regardless, his spiritual story and progression from paralyzing fear to freedom in grace is illuminating.

De Mello changed because he knew he was loved by another person; this energized him.[4] Martin Luther changed because he was willing to confront his fear of death and, in doing so, discovered the power of grace, which led him to a lasting faith.

The Wisdom of Jesus

The Christian tradition records an important story about Jesus that occurred near the end of his life. It is in all four gospels and is referenced in the Letter to the Hebrews.[5] It is the moment in Jesus' life when he was in anguish in the Garden of Gethsemane, just hours before his crucifixion and death. The gospel accounts place this event in the garden immediately after the Last Supper and just before the betrayal and arrest of Jesus. The story vividly illustrates both intimacy and vulnerability.

After withdrawing about a stone's throw from them and kneeling, he prayed, saying, "Father, if you are willing, take this cup away from me; still, not my will but yours be done." And to strengthen him an angel from heaven appeared to him. He was in such agony and he prayed so fervently that his sweat became like drops of blood falling

on the ground. When he rose from prayer and
returned to his disciples, he found them sleeping
from grief (Luke 22:41–45).

The intimacy between Jesus and his Father in heaven has been long established by this point in the gospel narratives. Jesus feels confident in his relationship with his Father, a truth referenced often in the New Testament. But despite the closeness, an intense agony and vulnerability is obvious in this passage. Jesus appears to be struggling with understanding the events that will soon unfold. He senses he is facing imminent death. If Jesus knew anything about his resurrection from the dead, that knowledge seems far away at this moment.

Of course, people far removed from the historical event itself know nothing of Jesus' personal psychology and inner thoughts. Most Scripture scholars agree that the words attributed to Jesus in the gospels most likely reflect the early Church's perspective on the episode rather than an eyewitness report. Yet, this crisp passage portrays a real sense of Jesus' anguish, suffering, and eventual surrender to the impending events.

It is what a person knows, not what a person does not know, that makes this encounter important and illustrative. In the anguish and struggle of Jesus in this moment, he knew of Abba's love for him, and he trusted him. He knew he had called people to a new way of seeing the world in which they lived. He knew the kingdom of God was already in their midst, although not yet fully engaged. He knew he had gathered people around him who seemed to be energized and inspired. He also knew he had left much undone and much incomplete. He did not know the details of what would happen next in the short term or in the long term. Would his efforts be enough? Would the mustard seed he had planted prosper and grow, or would it be trampled?

With these questions providing the background for his anguish, he was perhaps tormented with the prevailing Jewish viewpoint of death. All Jewish men and women perceived death as the place where there is no light and no life. It was the darkness of *Sheol*, where all people, whether good or evil, would wait for the final manifestation of God's promises to them. Would Jesus descend to *Sheol*, perceived and remembered as a man who was blessed by God or perceived and remembered [6] as a man cursed by God and abandoned?

Every fiber of Jesus' strength and commitment throughout his life, leading up to this moment, had been dedicated to fulfilling his Father's will. Nothing about any of Jesus' choices or actions during his life suggested he would waver, even for a moment, or would be capable of any hesitation. In this vivid memory and the story that remains from the experience, Jesus does cry out in torment and anguish. But he submits despite his fear. He submits to the will of his Father even if he does not fully comprehend it. The abandonment to death, and the complete emptying of his lifeblood in service to his Father's will, is testimony to his faith and trust.

Contextual Commentary

Let's return to the first pages of the Book of Genesis to one of the Creation stories that nourished the faith and imagination of a believing people. Called "pre-history" in biblical commentaries, it is helpful and revealing.

Now the snake was the most cunning of all the wild animals that the LORD God had made. He asked the woman, "Did God really say, 'You shall not eat from any of the trees in the garden'?" The woman answered the snake: "We may eat of the fruit of the trees in the garden; it is only about the fruit of the tree in the middle of the garden that God said, 'You shall not eat it or even touch it, or else you will die.'" But the snake said to the woman: "You certainly will not die! God knows well that when you eat of it your eyes will be opened and you will be like gods, who know good and evil." The woman saw that the tree was good for food and pleasing to the eyes, and the tree was desirable for gaining wisdom. So she took some of its fruit and ate it; and she also gave some to her husband, who was with her, and he ate it. Then the eyes of both of them were opened, and they knew that they were na-ked; so they sewed fig leaves together and made loincloths for themselves.

When they heard the sound of the LORD God walking about in the garden at the breezy time of the day, the man and his wife hid themselves from the LORD God among the trees of the gar-den. The LORD God then called to the man and asked him: Where are you? He answered, "I heard you in the garden; but I was afraid, be-cause I was naked, so I hid." Then God asked: Who told you that you were naked? Have you eaten from the tree of which I had forbidden you to eat? The man replied, "The woman whom you put here with me—she gave me fruit from the tree, so I ate it." The LORD *God then asked the woman: What is this you have done? The woman answered, "The snake tricked me, so I ate it" (Genesis 3:1–13).*

The ancient writer of Genesis proposes that the ability to see and understand is a gift that belongs exclusively to divinity. The writer mistrusts the experience of vulnerability between the man and the woman, insisting that their shared nakedness must be covered up. The writer also mistrusts the intimacy that had existed between man and woman and the presence of Divine Mystery. He opines in his story that humanity was secretly reluctant to believe that any kind of intimate relationship between humanity and divinity existed. Humanity, represented in this story by the first man and woman, was ripe for the plucking when the temptation was offered.

The writer seems to suggest that the original sin was not so much in the eating of the forbidden fruit (disobedience) but rather that the original man and woman were incapable of believing that there was a shared vision and life between humanity and divinity. Adam and

Eve were not cleverly manipulated by the serpent or deceived. What seems more plausible is that they blamed the serpent for helping them confirm what they already feared might be the truth deep within their hearts. They feared that they could not truly be intimate with God or appear in any way vulnerable to divinity. From the beginning, in the first moments of Creation, it seems that the fear of annihilation, the loss of self, was uppermost in their minds.

A traditional interpretation of this story places the emphasis on disobedience. However, in my opinion, to stress disobedience is to reduce the more helpful lesson on trust, vulnerability, and intimacy (the components of relationship). There is more mystery and more profound respect for the presence of the divine and the sacred in this story if readers resist the urge to reduce their acceptance of its truth to a single point: disobedience.

Disobedience as the primal cause of humanity's perceived separation and alienation from the presence of Divine Mystery may have made sense to a people rooted in patriarchy. It may have even made sense to the generations that followed and were steeped in the propaganda and stifling atmosphere of a society dominated by the divine right of kings. It does not make sense to people who are capable of a more enlightened interpretation. It does not make sense to people who are comfortable with more nuanced opinions that express a deeper mystery. The traditional narrow conclusion does not invite or enable a spiritually mature response to the sacred and holy.

If this contextual commentary gives you even a small bit of insight, the lesson may be that remaining connected to the spiritual journey is difficult work. It almost seems as if some instinct or behavior is knitted into the fabric of a person, providing a significant obstacle to entering and maintaining a relationship with the presence of Divine Mystery. If there is any hope of developing and nourishing this relationship, you should drink deeply from the authentic truth that can be found in the process of conversion. By starting to quench your thirst, you are slowly enabling your capacity to fearlessly embrace intimacy and vulnerability whenever possible.

Disconnect

Conversion depends on a person's ability to sustain both the discipline and the commitment that enable an environment of trust, intimacy, and vulnerability in his or her relationship with the presence of Divine Mystery. As in any relationship, such an environment is difficult to maintain. It requires constant vigilance, recommitment, and, perhaps most important in a spiritual relationship, a spiritual mentor or director who is willing to help the person sustain the necessary momentum. Conversion is vital.

To assert that a single point (conversion) is crucial to understanding, spiritual growth, and maturity is perhaps a bold statement. What evidence do I have, or is it just my opinion? I believe it is more than an opinion. To me, conversion is a basic point, and it has everything to do with being both religious and spiritual. Conversion, understood as the process that I've explained, is crucial because this intense and focused process of conversion is painful. As a person's opinions, judgments, perceptions, and even deeply held convictions are slowly stripped away, his or her inner vulnerability is exposed. For Divinity, the stripping away reveals sacredness and a glimpse into the mystery of the eternal. For humanity, the process reveals—not at all surprisingly, according to the witness of the Christian contemplative and mystical traditions—*almost the same experience.*

Although the revelation is in some manner identical,

there is a significant difference. A person does not easily recognize the mystery and the sacredness of who he or she is and was created to become. As a result of this inability to recognize the truth of what is fundamentally present, fear is revealed, and a nagging question of doubt lingers: can this profound experience possibly be true and authentic? At this point, a spiritual mentor or director who has encountered this same truth as part of his or her own spiritual journey is helpful. While a mentor or director cannot protect a person from doubt and confusion or shelter a person from the depth of feeling and emotion, he or she can help the person appreciate what is going on, maintain the required transparency, and put what the person is experiencing into some perspective.

If someone is undergoing conversion alone and unsupported, there is a great risk that he or she will disconnect from the experience. There is also the real possibility of disconnecting from the process even with the support of a spiritual director or mentor, but it's much less of a risk than going it alone.

Spiritual directors and mentors often observe that, during the conversion process, people have the tendency to switch directors or mentors. The individual senses that conversion is important and necessary, but he or she wants to avoid the pain. So, when the person experiences pain, he or she may mistakenly believe that something is missing in the relationship with his or her spiritual director or mentor and thus wants to find a "second opinion" or new direction. The impulse to switch gears is not unlike what people often feel when other relationships in life become difficult or challenging. The temptation is to "cut and run" or to seek a change.

An experienced spiritual director or mentor understands this tendency to disengage or to want a change. In such cases, the experienced, well-versed spiritual leader will gently but persistently try to provide more strength and guidance.

Spiritual direction or mentoring, although well intended and necessary, is occasionally misinterpreted by the person receiving it. In some cases, a person may incorrectly perceive spiritual direction as the director's desire to control or manipulate, which is almost never the case. A good spiritual director wants to guide and direct. People's perceptions and experiences, however, inform their discernment, and, when all is said and done, people will choose what they believe is best for them. The hope at this juncture is that directees will stay with their experienced directors or mentors and will be open to receiving their guidance.

There are numerous other ways for a person to disconnect at this point in the spiritual journey; for example, to take refuge in the written tradition of saints and sages. In the exchange between spiritual director and directee, the directee may present the director with opinions and teachings that are rooted in the developing spiritual tradition of centuries ago. Finding and clinging to a word, phrase, or directive taken out of its intended original context can be a powerful distraction that stops—hopefully only temporarily—a person's spiritual development. The experienced spiritual director or mentor will firmly but gently invite the person to continue progressing and to let go of whatever has gotten in the way.

Social media and the seemingly omnipresent "experts" have made the problems of confusion and distraction worse. Many of these people may be unaware that there are many spiritual traditions, practices, and preferences, even within a particular religious denomination. They don't know about the development of language, how one word might mean something in one century and something different at another time. They do not recognize the powerful presence of nuance and seem often to be blithely unaware of the theological struggles that are demonstrated daily on social-media platforms.

It can be hard to know whether a statement or talking point on social media is an opinion or an accurate representation of a spiritual tradition or practice. It also can be hard to know who are actual experts and who are charlatans who misrepresent their credentials or, worse, flat-out lie about who they are.

The conversion process is indeed fraught with difficulty and possible pitfalls, even for someone who is highly motivated. The process is agonizingly slow. It often plods along, one step at a time. Even the promise of future connections and a deeper, more substantially satisfying spiritual experience is sometimes not enough to keep a person going.

A friend who has attended many of my lectures, and who has been present on numerous occasions when I have presented this subject matter in a lecture format, consistently reacts strongly to the words of Sant Keshavadas in the introduction of this section. She dislikes the tone and the image of fear set forth by the words used by the saint to describe the consequence of entering into conversion. Yet, not to speak truthfully of the process and to avoid mentioning the difficulties would be disingenuous at best. I repeat the statement here to sum up, at least partially, this chapter.

> *Go ahead, light your candles and burn your*
> *incense and ring your bells and call out to God,*
> *but watch out, because God will come, and he*
> *will put you on his anvil and fire up his forge*
> *and beat you and beat you until he turns brass*
> *into pure gold.*

SANT KESHAVADAS

Chapter Five Notes

1. In some Christian spiritual traditions, the more appropriate word for this experience might be "surrender." I have chosen to retain the word "conversion" simply as a personal preference.

2. From Frederica Mathewes-Green: "Tradition calls the 'good thief' Dimas or Dismas, while the 'bad thief' is named Gestas. Dimas' legend reveals a little more. As a young man, he was the leader of a robber band in Egypt and encountered the Holy Family during their sojourn after Jesus' birth. He discerned something special about the Jewish family, we're told, and ordered his men to spare them. Thirty years later, he saw that child, as a man, nailed to a cross beside him."

3. The context of the story within the Gospel of Matthew immediately follows the question concerning what reward an apostle might expect (Matthew 19:27–30) and immediately precedes the request of the mother of Zebedee's sons for a position of power in the kingdom (Matthew 20:20–23). This placement seems to strengthen the interpretation of the parable in the manner in which I have presented it.

4. Peter G. Van Breemen, SJ, in his book *As Bread That Is Broken*, details perhaps one of the classic presentations of this experience in the first chapter: "The Courage to Accept Acceptance."

5. See Mark 14:32–42, Matthew 26:36–46, Luke 22:39–45, John 12:23–29, and Hebrews 5:7–10.

6. The record seems to clearly suggest that Jesus was very concerned with memory. "Do this in remembrance of me" (1 Corinthians 11:24) are his words, forever recalled and repeat-

ed in the Eucharist. "Remember me when you come into your kingdom" were the words of the thief on the cross next to him, words which prompted Jesus' generous response.

CHAPTER SIX

Resurrection
Living the Abundant Life

"The Great Way is not difficult for those who do not pick and choose. When preferences are cast aside, the Way stands clear and undisguised. But even slight distinctions made set earth and heaven far apart."

SENG-TS'AN, HSIN HSIN MING

"We should not prefer power to weakness, nor prefer health to sickness, wealth to poverty, pleasure to pain, this work to that one, and so it is with all things."

ST. IGNATIUS OF LOYOLA, *THE SPIRITUAL EXERCISES*

"Just as all things speak about God to those who know him, and reveal him to those who love him, they also hide him from all those who neither seek nor know him."

BLAISE PASCAL

"I begged for power and found it in knowledge.
I begged for honor and found it in poverty.
I begged for health and found it in asceticism.
I begged my account be lessened before God
     and found it in silence.
I begged for consolation and found it in despair."

ABOLHASSAN ALI EBN-E SAHL AZHAR ESFAHANI

"Abba Macarius while he was in Egypt discovered
a man who owned a beast of burden engaged in
plundering Macarius' goods. So he came up to the
thief as if he was a stranger and he helped him to load
the animal. He saw him off in great peace of soul,
saying, 'We have brought nothing into this world, and
we cannot take anything out of the world' (1 Timothy
6:7).

'The Lord gave and the Lord has taken away; blessed
be the name of the LORD' (Job 1:21).

SAYINGS OF THE DESERT FATHERS

Spiritual teachers and mentors from various traditions model and teach a truth that emerges from the discipline of contemplative living. People who are dedicated to a contemplative practice try to live each day with an attitude of accepting the gift of life as an opportunity for experiencing limitless possibilities. This stance is opposed to an attitude that life is constricted and often conflicted. Spiritual teachers also invite their students to spend time reflecting on the pivotal role that perception plays in framing an individual's interpretation of the meaning of life.

Perception is important, because what people think they see or understand is often the lens through which they interpret the meaning of life. For example, depending on perception, a person can see a glass of water as half-empty or half-full. It's the same glass, and the same amount of water. The only difference is how people perceive the glass and its contents.

Life teaches us that people sometimes resist accepting even the most basic truths. And accepted truths are sometimes ignored, forgotten, or misplaced. Thus, spiritual leaders try to remain focused and determined, not only for themselves but also for those who seek their expertise. They consistently call each spiritual sojourner back to an understanding that human judgments and opinions are formed primarily because of the perceptions that each person carries. Even with great effort and practice, changing your perception is difficult. People retain their way of seeing things because it is comfortable and familiar.

People form perceptions as the result of learned behavior, experience, culture, or any number of things. Unhelpful perceptions can lead people to believe illusions. "We see indistinctly, as in a mirror" (1 Corinthians 13:12). On the other hand, if people work through the process and grow in awareness daily, celebrate an awakened self, seek out silence and solitude, and permit the presence of Divine Mystery to mold them and change them, their perceptions can improve and become sharper. Contemplative living becomes a catalyst that permits and enables the fullness of life that people want to remain connected with.

A story told in the desert Southwest of the United States resonates with people who have lived or visited that part of the country, but everyone will get the message:

> *A man arrives home from work in the early evening. The sun is setting, and the shadows of the*

interplay between light and darkness cast their display of images all around him. He gets out of his car, walks up the path to his front porch, and freezes. There, on the front porch, curled and ready to strike, is a rattlesnake. The man, stopped still, perceives the danger before him. But as he stands frozen in place, the interplay of light and darkness continues to dance around him. After a few moments, his concerned wife flips on the porch light, and it illuminates the porch. He recognizes that the curled obstacle on his front porch is not a rattlesnake after all. It is his garden hose, exactly where he'd left it that morning.

The man in the story at first perceives danger, believing a rattlesnake was coiled and ready to strike. He assumes the posture of a man in immediate peril. However, as the light shines on his situation, he sees the truth. He begins to perceive the situation more clearly. What had caused him to freeze in place just moments before changed in an instant from a threat to life and safety into something harmless and useful.

Another powerful story about perception is found

in the Gospel of Matthew. The story highlights a single experience and compares the fundamental difference between the disciples' perception and the way Jesus effortlessly engages life. In the story, the disciples of Jesus perceive a scarcity while, in contrast, Jesus perceives abundance—"more than enough." It is a powerful story about changing perception and learning to see in the way suggested by the sacred and the mysterious.

When Jesus heard of it, he withdrew in a boat to a deserted place by himself. The crowds heard of this and followed him on foot from their towns. When he disembarked and saw the vast crowd, his heart was moved with pity for them, and he cured their sick. When it was evening, the disciples approached him and said, "This is a deserted place, and it is already late; dismiss the crowds so that they can go to the villages and buy food for themselves." [Jesus] said to them, "There is no need for them to go away; give them some food yourselves." But they said to him, "Five loaves and two fish are all we have here." Then he said, "Bring them here to me," and he ordered the crowds to sit down on the grass. Taking the five loaves and the two fish, and look-

ing up to heaven, he said the blessing, broke the loaves, and gave them to the disciples, who in turn gave them to the crowds. They all ate and were satisfied, and they picked up the fragments left over—twelve wicker baskets full. Those who ate were about five thousand men, not counting women and children.

MATTHEW 14:13–21

The apostles come to Jesus and point out the obvious: it is the dinner hour and the people who have gathered to listen to him are hungry. Their hearts and their spirits may well have been filled, but their stomachs are empty. The helpful apostles report to Jesus that there are more than 5,000 people to be fed. They also relay to Jesus with some urgency that the only food they can find for this enormous crowd of men, women, and children is five loaves of bread and two fish. In short, the apostles report to Jesus that "there is not enough." Jesus looks around and perceives something different. Despite the facts reported to him, he sees "more than enough." He knows that all he needs to do to relieve the apostles' concerns and feed the crowd is to reveal the abundance.

Jesus responds by inviting the people to sit down, blessing the food on hand, and directing everyone to share what has been blessed. Amazingly or perhaps even miraculously, the blessing produces enough nourishment for the hungry crowd—plus enough left over to feed many more! Jesus' blessing and invitation has freed the people from their fear and anxiety, anchored in their perception that "there is not enough." Jesus lifts the constraints of their limiting perception, and they now enjoy the abundance that has been in their midst from the start.

Originally, they were blind, unable to see clearly the reality surrounding them. As a direct response to Jesus and his blessing, they are invited into the light and enabled to see clearly. Scarcity is no issue. There is more than enough. There always has been enough. It just has been hidden away, protected, guarded, saved for when it is needed.

So often, when this story is retold and interpreted, the emphasis is on the miraculous: the miracle of multiplication. Although this interpretation is accurate, perhaps the miracle is in the revelation of the ordinary, not necessarily the extraordinary.

If we emphasize the extraordinary, the miracle performed by Jesus, then it seems to be an action or response that is entirely impossible for ordinary people. If, on the other hand, we emphasize the ordinary, then we recognize the power that comes from learning to see in a new way, and the event becomes more than simply a wonderful memory of what Jesus did. Understood in this manner, it becomes an experience that we can continually enjoy and celebrate, as well as something much, much more. The blessing, the sharing, the selfless giving—these are powerful examples of requirements for the Christian life: the life of the kingdom of God that is modeled by Jesus.

This story illustrates the profound difference between recognizing the abundance that is present and seeing only scarcity or the lack of something essential. In the former instance, the viewpoint modeled by Jesus, the people are presented with Jesus' vision of life, which shows them that everything they need is available to them. In the second instance, modeled by the apostles and the crowd, is the presumption that something is missing or at least in short supply.

What Jesus shows in this story—and in the example of his life—is so radically different from what seems to be the lived experience of many that it may seem impossible. However, when someone acknowledges the seemingly impossible and is willing to let his or her imagination run wild, if just for a moment, that person might recognize that the extraordinary experience of life could be the ordinary experience of life. When people give themselves permission to imagine and even believe, they can recognize the possibility of the kingdom of God. People of faith can learn to recognize the continuing possibility of the kingdom in the collective experience of humanity.

There is also an individual response to and acceptance of the kingdom of God: a daily living of the kingdom that is not dependent on the crowd but is a personal decision. Someone moving in response to the power of grace through the essential steps on the spiritual path can experience the abundance of God and reject a vision of life that sees only what is in short supply. The key is found in perception, in perseverance on the spiritual path, and in the language that the person uses to describe his or her experience.

Language—the words and phrases that people use to express themselves and their interpretations of their life experiences—is obviously a powerful force. The ability to communicate in complex sentences can effectively reveal not only someone's outer reality but also his or her inner reality. A person chooses words to accurately describe what he or she perceives at any given moment.

When experts in linguistics examine the workings of communication, they can clearly identify how people use language. Sentence structure, metaphors, figures of speech, and so forth—the choice of particular words and phrases, especially when they are consistently used by a person, reveals that person's perception of life.

In the story of the loaves and fishes, the apostles and disciples used words and syntax to communicate that there was not enough food; there was a scarcity of what they needed. Jesus, in contrast, effectively modeling the perception of someone steeped in the conviction of the kingdom of God, used different words and syntax to describe the same situation from the perspective of abundance. Comparing the words used by a person who observes the "lack of what is required" with the words used by a person who perceives that there is "more than enough" provides a valuable lesson and essential insight.

The language of scarcity is based on conditions, "shoulds," fears, anxieties, doubts, and other such human limitations. It is rooted in the condition that everything needs to be protected, measured, and parceled out. It's a language that will not give an inch, does not presume innocence, does not believe in forgiveness, demands justice, and is never satisfied, full, or complete. It is a language and a way of life based on the conviction that there is never enough.

The language of abundance is grounded in the belief that God is filled with plenty. It is the language of invitation, encouragement, confidence, gratefulness, and generosity. It is a language and an experience of life that has at its core the belief that love gives life, that forgiveness generates hope, and that all will be accomplished and fulfilled according to the plan of God. "My Father, if it is not possible that this cup pass without my drinking it, your will be done!" (Matthew 26:42).

The contrast between the language of scarcity and the language of abundance could not be more clearly illustrated. The reality of a human life marked by either perceived scarcity or perceived abundance could not be more starkly contrasted. There is an obvious choice and direction offered by this contrast, enabling people to recognize the invitation to a new way to live that is central to the teaching of Jesus and essential to Jesus' understanding of the kingdom of God.

In addition to the story of the loaves and fishes, there is a marvelous story in the Gospel of Luke that is pivotal for a deeper understanding of living life to the fullest—living a life of abundance in the kingdom of God. This well-known tale is the story of Emmaus.

> *Now that very day two of them were going to a village seven miles from Jerusalem called Emmaus, and they were conversing about all the things that had occurred. And it happened that while they were conversing and debating, Jesus himself drew near and walked with them, but their eyes were prevented from recognizing him. He asked them, "What are you discussing as you walk along?" They stopped, looking downcast. One of them, named Cleopas, said to him in reply, "Are you the only visitor to Jerusalem who does not know of the things that have taken place there in these days?" And he replied to them, "What sort of things?" They said to him, "The things that happened to Jesus the Nazarene, who was a prophet mighty in deed and word before God and all the people, how our chief priests and rulers both handed him over to*

a sentence of death and crucified him. But we were hoping that he would be the one to redeem Israel; and besides all this, it is now the third day since this took place. Some women from our group, however, have astounded us: they were at the tomb early in the morning and did not find his body; they came back and reported that they had indeed seen a vision of angels who announced that he was alive. Then some of those with us went to the tomb and found things just as the women had described, but him they did not see." And he said to them, "Oh, how foolish you are! How slow of heart to believe all that the prophets spoke! Was it not necessary that the Messiah should suffer these things and enter into his glory?" Then beginning with Moses and all the prophets, he interpreted to them what referred to him in all the Scriptures. As they approached the village to which they were going, he gave the impression that he was going on farther. But they urged him, "Stay with us, for it is nearly evening and the day is almost over." So he went in to stay with them. And it happened that, while he was with them at table, he took bread, said the blessing, broke it, and gave it to them. With that their eyes were opened and they recognized him, but he vanished from their sight. Then they said to each other, "Were not our hearts burning [within us] while he spoke to us on the way and opened the Scriptures to us?" So they set out at once and returned to Jerusalem, where they found gathered together the eleven and those with them who were saying, "The Lord has truly been raised and has appeared to Simon!" Then the two recounted what had taken place on the way and how he was made known to them in the breaking of the bread.

LUKE 24:13–35

Scripture scholars say this episode is pivotal to the formation of Jesus' disciples into a community of believers after his passion and death. It is a story that relates one of the ways that the disciples of Jesus were able to incorporate the teachings that would energize and animate the early Christian community.

The Emmaus story is about perception, embracing abundance, and refusing to be ensnared by an attitude of scarcity. It is fundamentally about moving out of the crippling grip of fear and anxiety generated by the violent death that Jesus suffered. It is not about death but rather about the courageous and faith-filled decisions that lead to life.

In the scene that the evangelist outlines in the gospel, the disciples welcome an unrecognized traveler in their midst. Once they welcome the stranger, they "break open" the Word of God in the Scriptures and celebrate the breaking of the bread in the eucharistic remembrance. This ritual action is a bold witness to their personal conviction of what will soon be revealed to them: meeting the resurrected Christ.

Welcoming a stranger in this time period was extraordinary. The pervasive attitude of the culture was to look upon an unknown person as "not one of us," and people viewed strangers with suspicion and distrust. In his ministry, Jesus welcomed all who were alienated and lived on the margins of society, consistently modeling a life that was countercultural. His constant practice of inclusion reversed the prevailing attitude of his time. At Emmaus, the disciples replicated Jesus' example, setting in motion an unpredictable outcome. The Emmaus story, in fact, became revelatory of a deeper and more profound mystery.

When the disciples break open the Word of God in the Scriptures, they engage a dynamic in which they are informed and led by the images, personalities, and stories of faith that are faithfully preserved in the written tradition. They enabled the Word of God to become a Living Word for them, not just a remembrance or a sterile record of a long time ago. Just as the presence of Divine Mystery was active and alive to their ancestors, the same relational experience continues in each person who opens their ears and their hearts to the Word of God.

When the disciples celebrate the breaking of the bread in the eucharistic remembrance of Jesus, they not only remember Jesus and his actions at the Last Supper, they also model the entirety of his teaching. *Everything that I modeled for you, do this in remembrance of me.*

This invitation to "living memory" goes beyond the simple action of sharing the bread and the cup. As each disciple begins to live a new way, he becomes a living memory of Jesus and sets out on a new path. In this new way of life, they choose to perceive the world around them as a movement out of the darkness and into the light. It is a movement from the prevailing culture of death to the resurrected life of the kingdom of God.

When the disciples boldly witness their personal convictions and experiences of the resurrected Christ, first to one another and then eventually to many other people, they become "I-witnesses" to the truth of the resurrection of Jesus, whom they loved and believed in as their Lord and teacher. In a sense, they proclaim, "Know that what I tell you, that the truth I witness to by my life, my choices, my actions, my judgments, and my desires is all the evidence you need to know and understand that I am living the Way and the Truth, which will lead to the life that you seek."

This response became perhaps the most effective model of evangelization in the early Christian community. This model, indicative of a profound spiritual maturity, provided both an individual and a communal framework for the proclamation of what each person, inspired by the teaching and the life of Jesus, understood as the movement from death to life and from darkness into light. This framework helped them deepen their commitment to enter into relationship with the presence of Divine Mystery, whom they understood as mysteriously incarnated in the person of Jesus.

The Wisdom of Jesus

The Gospel of Matthew, in describing the journey into the kingdom of God, contrasts the image of a wide door with the image of a narrow gate.

> *Enter through the narrow gate; for the gate is wide and the road broad that leads to destruction, and those who enter through it are many. How narrow the gate and constricted the road that leads to life. And those who find it are few.*
>
> MATTHEW 7:13–14

In Luke's Gospel, speaking again about how difficult it is to get into the kingdom of God, Jesus suggests that even if a person finds the "narrow door," that's not enough. An established relationship with the "owner of the house" is required for entry; a casual acquaintanceship won't do.

> *Strive to enter through the narrow door, for many, I tell you, will attempt to enter but will not be strong enough. After the master of the house has arisen and locked the door, then will you stand outside knocking and saying, "Lord, open the door for us." He will say to you in reply,*

"I do not know where you are from." And you will say, "We ate and drank in your company and you taught in our streets." Then he will say to you, "I do not know where [you] are from. Depart from me, all you evildoers!" And there will be wailing and grinding of teeth when you see Abraham, Isaac, and Jacob and all the prophets in the kingdom of God and you yourselves cast out. And people will come from the east and the west and from the north and the south and will recline at table in the kingdom of God. For behold, some are last who will be first, and some are first who will be last.

LUKE 13:24–30

Jesus' point is that the way to everlasting life in the kingdom of God is difficult. The teaching clearly underlines the toughness of the journey that leads to the narrow entrance. The struggle outlined in this story is even more striking when this teaching is seen in conjunction with other images that Jesus often uses to describe the experience of coming into the kingdom. The "blind guide" that leads his followers into the pit (Luke 6:39, Matthew 15:14), the "new patch of cloth" on the old garment that tears away, and the "new wine" into old wineskins (Matthew 9:16–17, Luke 5:36–38) are other examples that Jesus employs to illustrate his point.

Each example challenges people who encounter Jesus to favorably respond to his teaching. The stories stretch and pull people away from a perceived place of safety and comfort to the frontier of risking belief in something entirely new. As compelling as the examples are, there is one teaching that remains at the core of understanding what Jesus requires of those who are willing to be his disciples: "For whoever wishes to save his life will lose it, but whoever loses his life for my sake will find it" (Matthew 16:25). Thus, Jesus brings us face to face with our primal fear of death.

Most people fear death. Dying makes us confront helplessness, loss, and the possibility of personal annihilation. Death is the ultimate experience of scarcity, the moment when everything is taken away. Death seems to stand in contradiction to the abundant life of the kingdom of God.

Jesus faced death squarely, and he embraced becoming a victim. He breathed his last with the same fortitude of belief and conviction that animated his life, and, in so doing, Jesus dramatically repudiates the notion that death annihilates. The horror and public spectacle of his death impelled his apostles to incorporate his values and vision into their own lives and to face death. Their individual and collective witness—"He has risen!"—fuels the lifeblood of the community that was formed in his name, and it fuels Christians today.

The individual and collective refusal of Jesus' disciple-witnesses to live in fear was dramatic, even in the face of the prospect of an unspeakably violent death by crucifixion. They refused to be dragged back into helplessness, anxiety, and despair. Rather, they became living witnesses of what it means to let go of the poor substitute for life that scarcity believers endure and to live life believing in abundance, a sign of the kingdom of God. Each time these people responded "no" to signs of scarcity and lived fully and abundantly in the kingdom of God on earth, they had a resurrection: the new life Jesus promised.

The wisdom of Jesus and the challenge of his teaching propel people who believe in the promise of the resurrection well beyond the simplistic and stifling belief that resurrection is somehow limited to the experience of resuscitation. The fullness of resurrection is much more than just breathing life back into the human body.

When resurrection is reduced to resuscitation, the hope and promise of the teaching of Jesus are made thoroughly lifeless, becoming exactly what Jesus warned his disciples to avoid at all costs: the blind guide and the wide door that leads away from life and to destruction.

Contextual Commentary

Two pools, side by side, may provide a helpful illustration. One is a kiddie pool or a wading pool, no deeper than a foot. Next to it is a deeper swimming pool. At certain points, it is deep enough to dive into.

As you observe the pools, notice all the activity. Some people are splashing and swimming, having a wonderful time. Others are sitting on the side of the pool, just soaking their feet in the clear and inviting water. Some people are diving, while still others might be in the deepest part of the pool, exploring the bottom for hidden treasures or perhaps a lost coin. At first glance, the activity in both pools seems to be quite similar. A fair assumption might be that the people are using both pools for "swimming." That observation would be true, relatively speaking. There is, however, a significant difference between swimming in a wading pool and swimming in a pool that is much deeper.

Each pool symbolizes a different perspective about life and the spiritual journey. Further, each person using the pools may have different perceptions, opinions, and judgments about what it means to swim. Although they share the common experience of using a pool, there are points of divergence too.

A person whose life and beliefs are symbolized by the wading pool may be expending a lot of energy and seems to be fully engaged in what he or she is doing. However, the pool is very shallow, so this person may believe certain things about life that are true from his or her perspective but that are, in fact, extremely limiting. When someone's perspective suggests that resources (like the shallow water) are limited, he or she may strongly believe that those resources need to be measured, controlled, and parceled out.

If your life is symbolized by the deeper pool, you experience the ordinary and extraordinary events of life in a completely different manner. You won't feel that the resources needed for human existence need to be measured, controlled, or parceled out. For you, life is filled with abundance and possibilities.

The difference in perception and lived experience seen in the contrast between a wading pool and a deep swimming pool is not a matter of sinfulness, nor is it intended to reflect a lack of intelligence or goodwill. It is not even the consequence of a lack of imagination or creativity. It is, however, incomplete, at least from the perspective of the spiritual journey and growing in spiritual maturity.

This example can also illustrate the investment that people might make as they thoughtfully engage with the essential connecting points of the spiritual journey that we have discussed in this book. The more that people connect with each experience of relationship, practice and discipline, awareness and awakening, silence and solitude, conversion, and resurrection, the deeper their experience of the presence of Divine Mystery will be as it unfolds. It is simply and, at the same time, profoundly reflective of each individual's commitment to the spiritual journey and the development of spiritual maturity.

Disconnect

I occasionally watch *Hoarders*, a television show that has been on the A&E network since August 2009. The title of the show also bluntly describes the subject matter. It's a series that depicts the real-life struggles and treatment of people who suffer from compulsive hoarding. This program both attracts me and repels me. It attracts me because I am strangely fascinated by the quantity of stuff (for lack of a better word) that a single person can accumulate in consumer-centric American society. The program repels me because it is impossible not to feel the agony of the people who suffer from the compulsion to hold on to things. I don't find it entertaining to watch people suffer. It's not the suffering that attracts me to the show.

Each week, viewers witness someone's inability to determine the relative worth of a hamburger wrapper compared to the deed to a house. Paralyzed into inaction, the key player in the program keeps both "pieces of paper" in permanent storage, somehow perceiving each as treasures worth preserving. It is both fascinating and puzzling. The inability to decide, to discard that which is no longer useful, is similar to some of the choices and decisions we make in everyday life and in the spiritual life.

The "dis-ease" of the compulsive hoarder, and the result of hoarding, may be useful for illustrating a point of disconnect on the spiritual journey and the continuing growth into spiritual maturity. It may also be useful in reflecting upon "I am spiritual but not religious."

Living a life of abundance, which models the kingdom of God that Jesus preaches as essential for life, means that a person is convinced there is "more than enough." As a result of this lived conviction, the person has no need to store or fill their living space with things that can be accumulated, counted, stacked, numbered, or organized. Th accumulation of stuff includes not only household items, clothes, and trinkets but also—and more to the point—ideas, opinions, perceptions, judgments, definitions, dogmas, doctrines, life experiences, blessings, and disappointments. In short, everything that a person may count as important and necessary.

This is not to say that these things are not helpful, nor that a person surrounded by such things will not use them. Rather, it is a powerful belief that a person should not be attached to things in a manner that defines his or her self-worth and importance. The ability to remain unattached amid abundance is one of the keys to spiritual maturity and, as such, a possible point where a disconnect can occur.

Meister Eckhart,[1] a Dominican theologian and writer in the late thirteenth and early fourteenth centuries, is acclaimed by many as one of the greatest German mystics. He was completely dedicated to contemplative living. In the transcripts of his sermons in German and Latin, he charts the course of union between the individual soul and the presence of Divine Mystery. In a work titled *Theological Expressions*, he espouses pertinent thoughts in a poignant summary:

> *The only thing that burns in hell is the part of you that won't let go of your life: your memories, your attachments. They burn them all away, but they're not punishing you, they're freeing your soul. If you're frightened of dying and you're holding on, you'll see devils tearing your life away. If you've made your peace, then the devils are really angels freeing you from the earth.*

The stored objects, ideas, thoughts, opinions, and whatever else we might manage to lock in our grip will be stripped away when we die. Eckhart's description of the process invites us to consider another possibility: If a person is seeking freedom and life, then the stripping away begins when the person freely loosens his or her grip and resists the urge to hoard and accumulate, resting in the conviction that there is "more than enough." It is a painful process, but in one scenario, stripping away leads to chosen freedom; in the other, perhaps more painful scenario, freedom is imposed.

The temptation to disconnect from the spiritual journey and to settle for an action that distracts is powerful. No single man or woman is exempt from the temptation to accumulate.

As it is in human life, so it is with institutions, including those established for important and necessary purposes and missions, such as religion. For example, some institutions that have existed for centuries retain laws, procedures, and customs that are no longer meaningful or effective but are still on the books. Such institutions, perhaps because of their perceived importance, are sometimes reluctant to strip away that which is unnecessary, time-worn, or even counterproductive. Over time, these institutions can be perceived as guardians and protectors of what has been accumulated rather than what is required and relevant, which may overwhelm their foundational and intended purposes.

Accumulation, storage—the need to secure and protect—and all other manifestations of what it means to hold on dearly to something, whatever it may be, become effective distractions from the commitment needed to maintain a relationship. This is true in all relationships, including the relationship between a person and the presence of Divine Mystery.

To help illustrate this point is a story is from the Suffi tradition of wisdom stories. The central character is Nasruddin, a sage who is sometimes seen as a bumbling fool in such stories. Nevertheless, he teaches a valuable lesson—in this instance, the futile effort to secure, protect, and accumulate for a later date.

> *Nasruddin had a little money. He wanted to hide it somewhere. At first, he dug a hole, kept the money there, and covered it with soil. After a while, he thought the money would be discovered soon and was not safe there. So, he dug another hole and kept the money there. He repeated this many times, but he was still not sure that his money was secure.*

> *He took the money from its last hiding place, put it a bag, and rode on a donkey to take the bag to a hilltop near his house. He fixed a stick vertically in the ground and suspended the bag from it. Looking at it from a distance, Nasruddin commented, "A human being is not a bird to come here and steal the bag." He went back home.*

A man who was watching Nasruddin from a distance took the money from the bag and poured the dung of a camel into the bag. After a few days, when Nasruddin needed money, he went to find the bag. When he brought the bag down from the stick, he found the dung of a camel in it. Surprised, he said, "This is very interesting. How could a camel reach a place where a person could not?"

People don't dissociate from religious practices because they lack spirituality. They do so because they are repelled by what religion has accumulated, hoards, defends, and keeps collecting. People are convinced this way of living rewards scarcity, not abundance. This is especially true when religion places an emphasis on who is acceptable and who is not.

It seems to me that a person who is walking a spiritual path believes in mystery and expects to be surprised daily by the manifestation of the Divine. For a spiritual person and for a person who practices a specific religion, there must always be an openness to life. There must be a willingness to take in the light and let go of the darkness. Above all, people on the spiritual path must celebrate the abundance of all that surrounds them instead of giving in to the temptation to emphasize that which is in short supply.

To once again paraphrase Julian of Norwich and to take some liberties with what she so often proclaimed as a person of the light: Enter the mystery and all will be well!

Chapter Six Notes

1. His original name was Johannes Eckhart. He was also called Eckhart von Hochheim (circa 1260–1327). This quote was compiled for use in the movie *Jacob's Ladder*, a 1990 psychological thriller.

Afterword

It might be difficult to imagine, but I can remember a sermon that I was privileged to listen to more than forty-five years ago as a young seminarian. I sat in the Redemptorist Seminary Chapel of St. Joseph's Preparatory College in Edgerton, Wisconsin, attending daily Mass. The priest celebrant and preacher that day was Rev. Robert Reitcheck, CSsR. Because of the difficulty of pronouncing his last name correctly, we students and the priests and brother on campus called him, affectionately, "Fr. Bob." On this day, Fr. Bob was in fine form. In fact, "fine form" was not unusual for a man of his talent and ability, as I learned in the months and years that followed.

Fr. Bob started his sermon by asking his listeners to go with him on a journey. Our "destination" was the attic of an old country home in the township of Angelus in Sheridan County, Kansas. This place, well known to Fr. Bob because it was where he spent his youth, intrigued me. I had never been to Kansas, and the thought of an attic in this exotic place with the spiritual name "Angelus" was exciting.

As I closed my eyes and followed his directions, my excitement increased. He instructed us to climb the stairs that led to the second floor of the farmhouse. He continued by requiring us, his listeners, to pause at the top of the stairs, all the while looking up to discover the pull-down ladder concealed in the attic's ceiling. With each instruction and new discovery, I could feel my anticipation increasing. What were we going to find? What was so important that needed securing in this secret place?

When I and my companions on this journey, the student body and some of the faculty who had given themselves permission to indulge their imagination, finally "gathered" in the attic of the house, our intention was tightly focused. At least mine was. There, in the middle of the attic, was an old steamer trunk, the focus of our journey. Fr. Bob said it was covered with dust and bore the remnants of old luggage tags that identified trips and adventures long since completed and, perhaps, forgotten.

Fr. Bob continued by explaining how, as a young boy and even into manhood, he would disappear into the attic on cold days when there was nothing else to do. There, he would gently open the trunk and slowly, gently pull back the protective layers of gingham cloth that protected the contents.

As Fr. Bob talked, he showed us what he saw. Sure enough, in front of his eyes and ours, treasures of long ago slowly came into view. Old photographs of family and friends; a neatly folded infantry uniform from World War I; a little black box with Army medals of service and honor; a white wedding dress, so delicate and fragile that it was difficult to believe anyone could have worn it; a family Bible, tucked into a corner of the trunk, filled with holy cards to mark significant passages from the Scriptures. He uncovered his bronzed baby shoes, the kind that now appear at antique shows. He found wheat, flowers, and leaves—all of which once swayed back and forth gracefully in the winds of the Great Plains of Kansas—that had been pressed between the pages of an ancient album for safe keeping.

As Fr. Bob continued, I could feel the meaning of each image, the power of each treasure revealed. Each moment of history that the ordinary yet precious objects represented spoke volumes about life and love, strength and weakness. But perhaps most of all, as the priceless mementos were laid out in front of his audience that day, they revealed the character of the people who once lived in this old farmhouse in the middle of Kansas— country folk who dared to name their township "Angelus." I understood that this unassuming trunk housed much more than assorted memories. To me, it was clear that each item bore witness to the sacred, the spiritual, and the mysterious. This worn steamer trunk was as grand as any cathedral. It witnessed to the presence of God.

As the pages of this reflection come to their conclusion, it may be appropriate to end where I began, on the windswept plains of the ancient Holy Land with humanity's ancestors in faith, Abraham and Sarah. As they learned and progressed on their spiritual path, and as they experienced the movement from awareness to awakening in each of their encounters with the presence of Divine Mystery, I hope you discovered the seeds of the spiritual journey of those who have followed in their footsteps. In the events and the experiences of each of their lives, they were invited to a new way of seeing and a world of unlimited possibilities. For Abraham and Sarah, their own abundance and limitless possibilities are recorded for the ages in the Book of Genesis:

> *[The LORD] took him outside and said: Look up at the sky and count the stars, if you can. Just so, he added, will your descendants be. Abram put his faith in the LORD, who attributed it to him as an act of righteousness. He then said to him: I am the LORD who brought you from Ur of the Chaldeans to give you this land as a possession.*

GENESIS 15:4–7

For Abraham and Sarah, their relationship with the presence of Divine Mystery was symbolized by God's promise of countless descendants and the richest land for grazing and living imaginable. It is this abundance that would appeal to a Bedouin nomad but perhaps not to people in the twenty-first century. Perhaps today, for a person who lives in a consumption-driven culture, where men and women of the developed world are surrounded with more choices than they can count, the promise of abundance is uninspiring and perhaps meaningless. That's to be expected.

However, the promise of a life that is unburdened, a life that enables each person to see a clear vision and purpose, a life that integrates instead of separates, may well appeal to the people of this age. Unquestionably, God's promise to the spiritual seekers Abraham and Sarah and that vow's awe-inspiring fulfillment in the centuries after is dramatic, simple, and mysterious. In the presence of Divine Mystery, in the daily life in the kingdom of God, the promise becomes a reality for all those who accept the invitation to seek, to learn, and then to practice a new way of seeing, a new way of living, and a new way of believing each and every day.

May God bless you on your journey.

Earth's crammed with heaven,
And every common bush afire with God:
But only he who sees, takes off his shoes.

—ELIZABETH BARRETT BROWNING,
AURORA LEIGH

Bibliography

Bhikkhu, Thānissaro. *The Wings to Awakening: An Anthology of the Pali Canon*. 4th ed. Barrie, MA: Dhamma Dana Publications, 2004.

Browning, Elizabeth Barrett. *Aurora Leigh*. Oxford, England: Oxford University Press, reissued 2008.

Catechism of the Catholic Church, 2nd ed. Washington, DC: United States Conference of Catholic Bishops, 2016.

Conservapedia. https://www.conservapedia.com/St._Thomas_Aquinas

Crossan, John Dominic, and Jonathan L. Reed. *Excavating Jesus: Beneath the Stones, Behind the Texts*. New York: HarperCollins, 2001.

Darnell, Eric, and Tim Johnson, dirs. *Antz*. Glendale, CA: DreamWorks Animation and Pacific Data Images, 1998.

de Mello, Anthony, SJ. *Awareness: Conversations with the Masters*. New York: Doubleday, 1990.

———. The Song of the Bi. *The Song of the Bird*. New York: Doubleday, 1984.

Diamond, Neil. *Beautiful Noise*. Columbia Records, 1976.

Doyle, Brendan. *Meditations with Julian of Norwich*. Santa Fe, NM: Bear and Company, 1986.

Gittins, Anthony J. *A Presence that Disturbs: A Call to Radical Discipleship*. Liguori, MO: Liguori Publications, 2002.

Hammarskjöld, Dag. *Markings: Spiritual Poems and Meditations*. London: Faber & Faber, 1973.

Hanh, Thich Nhat. *Living Buddha, Living Christ*. New York: Riverhead Books, 1995.

Haskins, Susan. *Mary Magdalen: Myth and Metaphor*. New York: HarperCollins, 1993.

Herbert, Frank. *Dune*. New York: Ace Books, 1999.

Holt, Bradley R. *Thirsty for God: A Brief History of Christian Spirituality*. Minneapolis: Fortress Press, 2005.

Jäger, Willigis. *Contemplation A Christian Path*. Liguori Publications/Triumph Books, 1994.

Johnson, Elizabeth A., CSJ. *Quest for the Living God: Mapping Frontiers in the Theology of God*. London: Continuum, 2007.

Juergensmeyer, Mark. *Terror in the Mind of God: The Global Rise of Religious Violence*. Berkeley, CA: University of California Press, 2017.

Kornfield, Jack. *After the Ecstasy, the Laundry: How the Heart Grows Wise on the Spiritual Path*. New York: Bantam, 2001.

Ladinsky, Daniel. *Love Poems from God: Twelve Sacred Voices for the East and West*. London: Penguin Books, 2002.

Marius, Richard. *Martin Luther: The Christian Between God and Death*. Cambridge, MA: Belknap Press, 2000.

Merton, Thomas. *New Seeds of Contemplation*. New York: New Directions, 2007.

———. *What Is Contemplation?* Springfield, IL: Templegate Publishers, 1981.

The New American Bible, Revised Edition. Division of Christian Education of the National Council of the Churches of Christ in the USA, 2010.

Pagola, José Antonio. *Jesus: An Historical Approximation.* Miami: Convivium Press, 2009.

Pantheism.net

Pope Francis. *The Joy of the Gospel: Evangelii Gaudium.* Washington, DC: United States Conference of Catholic Bishops, 2013.

Redemptorist Pastoral Publication. *The Essential Catholic Handbook.* Liguori, MO: Liguori Publications, 1978.

Rodriguez, Otilio, translator. *St. Teresa of Ávila: The Collected Works, Vol. I.* Washington, DC: ICS Publications, 1985.

Rolheiser, Ronald. *The Holy Longing: The Search for a Christian Spirituality.* New York: Doubleday, 1999.

Sagan, Carl. *Pale Blue Dot: A Vision of the Human Future in Space.* New York: Ballantine Books, 1997.

Sedlak, Kenneth, CSsR, Unpublished exercise from Pathways learning community. St. Michael's, 2003.

Seligman, Adam B. *Modernity's Wager: Authority, the Self, and Transcendence.* Princeton, NJ: Princeton University Press, 2000.

Tickle, Phyllis. *The Great Emergence: How Christianity Is Changing and Why.* Ada, MI: Baker Books, 2008.

Tolle, Eckhart. *Stillness Speaks.* Novato, CA: New World Library, 2003.

Uhlein, Gabriele. *Meditations with Hildegard of Bingen.* Santa Fe, NM: Bear and Company, 1983.

Van Biema, David, "Mother Teresa's Crisis of Faith," *Time*, August 23, 2007.

Van Breemen, Peter G., SJ. *As Bread that Is Broken.* Denville, NJ: Dimension Books 1974.

Wilber, Ken. *A Theory of Everything: An Integral Vision for Business, Politics, Science, and Spirituality.* Boulder, CO: Shambhala Publications, 2000.

Woodruff, Sue. *Meditations with Mechtild of Magdeburg.* Santa Fe, NM: Bear and Company, 1982.